LOOKING AT, TALKING ABOUT, AND LIVING WITH CHILDREN

Reflections on the Process of Schooling

Russell L. Dobson
Judith E. Dobson
J. Randall Koetting
Oklahoma State University

UNIVERSITY
PRESS OF
AMERICA

LANHAM • NEW YORK • LONDON

4720 Boston Way
Lanham, MD 20706

3 Henrietta Street
London WC2E 8LU England

Library Congress Cataloging-in-Publication Data

Dobson, Russell.
   Looking at, talking about, and living with children.

   Includes bibliographical references and index.
   1. Education—United States—Curricula.
2. Educators—United States—Language—Psychological
aspects. 3. Curriculum planning—United States—
Philosophy. 4. Teachers—United States—Attitudes.
I. Dobson, Judith Shelton.   II. Koetting, J.
Randall. III. Title.
LB1570.D58   1985   375'.001'0973   85-11237
ISBN 0-8191-4786-9 (alk. paper)
ISBN 0-8191-4787-7 (pbk. : alk. paper)

All University Press of America books are produced on acid-free
paper which exceeds the minimum standards set by the National
Historical Publications and Records Commission.

To our children

Mark, Mike, Susan, Steve

John, Susan

Joshua, Katherine, Johanna

ACKNOWLEDGEMENTS

In the preparation of this book, the authors are grateful to many people for their assistance. They are particularly indebted to the students in their classes at Oklahoma State University, whose cooperation made possible a thorough trial of the concepts. Special credit goes to Ms. Dianne Wimberley, Ms. Allene Tonips, and Ms. Dana Marie Milligan who went far beyond their duties in typing and editing the manuscript, to participating in its development by serving as advisors and supportive friends.

v

TABLE OF CONTENTS

PREFACE

This book is written for those who are responsible for the education of the young, with the hope the content might encourage speculation. The book is written especially for those who are not satisfied with the prevailing technological approach being used almost exclusively to deal with educational complexities which are social, ethical, and political in nature.

This is a book about curriculum and teaching. The focus is on everyday life in schools. Admittedly, such a broad area is difficult to consider in its entirety. However, this is a large part of what we consider to be a major problem in education--extensive analysis of the "parts" abstracted from the "whole." In seeing parts of schooling in isolation from the "whole," educational theorists and practitioners have offered simplistic responses to complex problems. A sophisticated technical rationale of education has resulted which appeals to and promotes commonsense notions of schooling.

There is a growing concern on the part of the public that the quality of education provided for the young in American schools is declining. We share this concern. However, our concerns are different from those being promoted. Some writers advance rhetoric relative to an urgency to improve declining academic scores, the lack of discipline, classroom management, teacher competence, and the like. Our concern is with the freedom of each child; the inalienable right of all children to reach toward their unlimited potential to love, to create, to learn, to grow.

During the past decade, the literature in the field of education receiving primary attention has turned away from the notion of the fully functioning person toward a viewpoint that is based on prediction, control, and manageability: students in their proper places doing the appropriate things. The political, ethical, and aesthetic realities evolving from this mentality, although overwhelming, generally go unquestioned by educational theorists and practitioners.

We are apprehensive about the exaggerated dependence on a technocratic-rationale to improve the schooling experience of the young. This dependence leads to a human dilemma existing in schools as well as other bureaucracies. How can a person (teacher, student) express and maintain self in a social environment (school) demanding accommodation to an established norm?

The use of a technocratic-rationale in attempts at educational improvement have primarily taken the form of a production model. The young are processed through 13 years of public school in the same manner that Henry Ford built the Model T, using an assembly line. The major goal of this model is to manufacture a standard product. The quality check is one of utility according to a predetermined function. The over-dependence on technocratic-rationale has resulted in a school experience designed according to an industrial model which has, as its major goal, designing humans to become standardized instruments of society. All of this is done from an utilitarian perspective.

In spite of claims by proponents of movements such as accountability, behavioral objectives, competency-based testing, and teaching effectiveness research, the school experience of youngsters has not improved appreciably. In some instances it appears the unwillingness to critically examine technocratic-rationale has reached an epidemic stage. If we expect schools to improve, then this pathological preoccupation must be tempered.

It is not enough to continue to debate or to think about schooling from a perspective of amelioration. There certainly is no shortage of this activity. Sometimes in order to improve or provide alternatives to a phenomenon it becomes necessary to revisit, revitalize, and reconstruct the concepts forming the basis for that phenomenon. This requires new ways of thinking and talking. The basic concepts and language used by curriculum and instruction experts in designing schooling are subject to critique. Hopefully, new ways of thinking and talking about humans in conjunction with the schooling experience will result in new ways of treating them. The essays in this book are written not only from the standpoint of taking issue with much of what is happening in schools, but with the intent of calling attention to the casualness or ease with which decisions about curriculum and instruction are being made.

In Chapters 1 and 2 we take a critical look at the ways the school as a social institution might be promoting an ideology of control instead of a model of freedom and democracy, demanded by our constitution. Chapter 1 attends specifically to the power of perception and language as tools to use in examining and reconceptualizing the school experience. In Chapter 2 we provide a critical analysis of the practice of homogenization as an attempt to standardize the product (student). In Chapter 3 we attempt to bring clarity to confusion by presenting a model for curriculum dialogue whereby educators can come together to engage in responsible "talk" relative to the purpose of schooling the young. Chapters 4 and 5 present a critical analysis of teacher effectiveness research grounded in a technocratic-rationale model. In this model, teaching is viewed as a managerial function devoted to manufacturing a product. Chapters 6 through 8 present alternatives to this dominant model currently used to design schooling experiences by emphasizing areas needing further analysis and refinement. The content of the essays also provides a basis for immediate action. Although it has become habit in certain educational circles to so believe, it does not logically follow that if one raises criticism about a phenomenon he/she is obligated to provide an alternative or solution. Our intent in Chapters 6 through 8 is not to provide solutions to the criticisms raised in Chapters 1 through 5, but rather to present the results of our efforts at reconceptualization.

x

As the reader proceeds through this book it becomes increasingly evident that a particular set of values has been endorsed. That was our intent. Unlike some educators, we do not see value-neutrality as prerequisite to scholarly endeavor. A further intent is to suggest that those who make educational decisions spend time and effort examining the philosophic and political roots of critical educational issues and problems. We hope the content of the book might serve as a catalyst for responsible educators to begin examining, understanding, and developing basic systems of philosophy, as well as understanding relationships, ethical and logical, between certain educational points of view and day-to-day school methodology and procedures. Through this process, we hope educators demonstrate a higher level of sophistication in becoming more sensitive to and aware of biases involved in recommendations and/or pressure to subscribe to current fads and trends in curriculum and instruction. Responsible educators, in attempting to survive, cannot continue to ignore what is quietly going on in their heads while they assume a reactive posture to external impositions. Our goal in writing this book is to encourage educators to reflect upon and listen to their internal manifestations of ethical and aesthetic considerations about the schooling of the young.

RLD
JED
JRK
Stillwater, Oklahoma
May, 1985

SECTION I

STATE OF THE ART: THE HIDDEN CURRICULUM AS A NEGLECTED FORCE

Much of the activity of curriculum theorists and practitioners has its derivation in conventional wisdom, a perspective with questionable validity. Apple (1975a, p. 121) refers to this wisdom as "habits of thought ...a taken-for-granted reality that has become so commonsensical that we have ceased to even question it." We assert in the next two chapters that the epistemological base of current practices in American schools is enjoying a virtually unquestioned and unchallenged position. The market on encapsulation seems to have been cornered. What is real and what is reality continue to be treated as if they were synonymous phenomena.

Ideas, unformed conceptions, are inventions of human agents. Curriculum theorists conceive as well as collect ideas from established disciplines and arrange them in various structures in order to create concepts unique to education. These concepts exist in the human mind and are used not only to affirm reality, but as tools to create educational thought. Additionally, certain concepts are clustered by curriculum theorists to represent a particular perspective of human life or culture, resulting in an ideology. Thus, curriculum thought and activity is ideologically based. If concepts are syntheses of selected ideas, and ideas are inventions of human agents, then the potential for epistemological error exists. In order to adequately critique curriculum knowledge, it is not enough to examine the knowledge itself. It also becomes necessary to examine the way in which the knowledge was created. This can only be done by examining the conceptual base used in its formulation.

The major theme of this section of the book suggests the epistemological base of much curriculum and instruction practice is grounded in logical positivism and thus conceptually limited. By limited we mean bound, eliminating the possiblity of going beyond what is currently thought to be known.

Logical positivism has had a tremendous impact on the theory, research, and practice of curriculum in the past two decades (e.g., management by objectives, competency-based testing, accountability movement, competency-based teacher education and diagnostic, prescriptive treatment). Basically, logical positivism is a blending of symbolic logic and the scientific method (validation through experience). Auguste Comte and other forerunners of the movement believed that symbolic logic could be used to construct systems and that through a process of reductionism, general laws could be reduced to propositions which could be established through scientific verification, thus establishing reality. This procedure is commonly referred to as a reductionist perspective. Its advocates can be accused of dealing with particulars out-of-context. Logical positivists, for the most part, tend to ignore epistemological questions dealing with the metaphysical, theological, and ethical.

Historically, logical positivists believed that knowledge about natural phenomena was knowledge about human phenomena. This has resulted in a value-free science in which some curriculum theorists believe that objectivity and neutrality are necessary ingredients when establishing school programs of fairness and equality.

An additional result of this positivistic activity has been the encouragement of a technical rationale. The goal is to create knowledge that can be used to predict and control both natural and human phenomena; thus, when dealing with humans, an instrumental metaphor becomes appropriate. The human is viewed as an instrument to be shaped and molded to fit into the "proper scheme of things." Logical positivistic practices have a controlling effect. Many school functions tend to reflect this ideology of control (e.g., labeling, homogenous grouping, tracking, positive reinforcement, emphasis on correct behavior, and the grading system). This list of examples demonstrates an almost pathological preoccupation with managing human behavior in a school setting which may or may not create the conditions necessary for optimal cognitive and affective development of children and youth.

In Chapter 1 we build a case that the language and values used to design the schooling experience serve to perpetuate and intensify this technocratic-rationale. In Chapter 2 we present an analysis of how schools, built on an epistemological base of logical positivism, may be severely limited in designing learning situations.

In this opening chapter we want to emphasize the necessity of examining the power of words (languaging). We believe this to be a neglected phenomenon in the field of education. The way educators look at (perceive), talk about (language), and live with (experience) children is an area worthy of critical analysis. We will present a set of assumptions relative to perception and language, along with a discussion of the interplay of perceptions, language, and values, and their attendant effects on the educational experiences of children. We conclude the chapter by providing an alternative orientation, based in aesthetic and ethical values, for looking at, talking about, and living with children.

CHAPTER I

LOOKING AT, TALKING ABOUT, AND LIVING WITH CHILDREN*

Fantasize for a moment that you are traveling to a particular mountain for a backpacking trip. You become aware of the mountain as it comes into view. You have seen other mountains or pictures of mountains, and you have studied about mountains in school where you learned the appropriate label (word) for the object. Upon arrival and while preparing for your backpacking trip, you experience this mountain: the temperature, sounds (wind, leaves rustling, quietness), and fragrance (pine needles, clean air).

During the hike up the trail, you become more aware of this mountain's uniqueness. Discovering a variety of wild flowers or colorful mushrooms encourages lingering moments for inspection and awe. The trail crosses streams with tumbling waterfalls and small pools which seem to capture the rays of the sun at just the right moment and angle. Perhaps you catch a glimpse of a deer or other animal. Camping for several days at a lake encourages rest and reflection. When departing from the mountain and glancing back for a last "look," you see something quite different from your original view. You have experienced this particular mountain; it has become a part of your perceptual base. When attempting to share your perceptions and experiences with friends, words do not seem to capture the magic of the adventure. If you are unable to express this total experience with the mountain, then why expect more of words when speaking of children and the schooling experience?

If a teacher is asked to describe a particular child, the description (communication) will be given in words, either written or oral. The worth of the report and the competence of the teacher often are assessed by the technical language used. Technical reports by professionals tend to "fix" humans in their enviornments. Appignanesi (1976, p. 40) states, "...words not so much used, as poured like concrete: so that they become, literally, unthinkable."

The power of words (languaging) is probably the most overlooked, least understood, and ultimately most neglected phenomenon in the field of education. Words serve to produce a paradoxical situation: both the freezing and unfreezing of reality. With the technical emphasis in the field of education on the operational definition of terms along with the use of observable behavior to explain the human condition, words tend to provide more of a freezing function. Apple (1975b), Freire (1970) and

---

*This chapter is a revised version of our article which appears in The Journal of Curriculum Theorizing, IN PRESS.

Wesker (1976) suggest language is not passive or neutral. Either we use language justly or we will be badly used by it.

Educators invent words to serve as tools and their perceptions become controlled by these creations. Lanugage which is intended to explain or describe reality becomes reality. What can't be explained (or for that matter programmed into the computer) is too often ignored and ultimately dismissed. We are suggesting that the way we talk about a phenomenon determines what we see before we look. The language of a field encourages human encounters to be a priori. If we are to pursue the reality of the teaching-learning act, educators must uncover the meanings of words blurred by custom and usage.

More than half a century ago, E. K. Wickman (1929) concluded from his studies on teacher perception of children's behavior that no act of misbehavior had been committed until someone judged it as such. Assuming the validity of this premise, it seems reasonably safe to assume the opposite. No act of appropriate behavior has been committed until someone has judged it as such. The reporting of perception (reality) requires judgement which in turn reflects the value posture of the one doing the reporting.

The non-neutrality of methods of inquiry has been argued by Habermas (1971). Contrary to his argument, the encouraged mode of perception in teaching is one of value-neutrality in the form of observation. Certain behavioral characteristics of children are classified and labeled and teachers are trained to see these. This activity has resulted in the field of teacher education abounding with an "if-then" mentality, a reduction of the cause-effect model borrowed from natural science. If a child exhibits a certain behavior, then an appropriate treatment is prescribed. Apple (1979) points out that educators have borrowed the reconstructed logic of science and applied it to curriculum and pedagogical research and practice.

Patterns of thought or the usage of language schemes borrowed from the natural sciences simply do not fit summarily the social sciences. Exactness and precision are needed when dealing with things (natural sciences) for purposes of prediction and control. However, latitude and flexibility are needed when dealing with humans for purposes of growth, evolvement, emancipation, and understanding.

If the cause-effect model borrowed from the natural sciences were transferable in its entirety to the social sciences, then economists would predict inflation and interest rates, and political scientists could accurately forecast election outcomes. If the model is not applicable in those social sciences that lend themselves to exactness, why have educators become so infatuated with the power of the cause-effect concept in the study of children? The ultimate thrust of the cause-effect model is prediction and control; emancipation and understanding are secondary concerns.

6

Apple (1975a, p.127) contends that "...two major problems in education historically have been our inability to deal with ambiguity, to see it as a positive characteristic, and our continual pursuit of naive and simplistic answers to complex human dilemma." He continues by suggesting that phenomenologists seek to cast aside their previous perceptions of familiar objects and attempt to reconstruct them. The work of the phenomenologist is to see the phenomenon as it is rather than as it is suggested. The basic question becomes one of whether or not "familiar" educational constructs for viewing and speaking of children are adequate relative to the potential of children.

Tranel (1981) supports Apple's contention about educators' unwillingness to deal with ambiguity when he states:

The cause and effect model was first discredited in physics by Heisenberg's conception in 1927 of the "uncertainty principal." If, therefore, this model is inapplicable in the world of material substances, it is all the more inappropriate and misleading in the unique world of the individual, where measurement and predicitability are inherently precluded. (p. 425)

Professionals must deal not only with what they see but with <u>why they see what they see.</u> This is a simple notion, just simple enough to be almost totally overlooked and neglected. The way educators look at (perceive), talk about (language), and live with (experience) children is an area worthy of critical analysis. In the remainder of this chapter we present a set of assumptions relative to perception and language and provide a model for explaining the interplay of perceptions, language, and values and the effects of certain mixes on the educational experiences of children. We conclude by providing an alternate model for looking at, talking about, and living with children.

Assumptions

1. The way educators talk (word usage) affects what they see (perceptions). This phenomenon also works in a reciprocal fashion. Causal priority does not seem particularly important.

2. Perceptions and language are reflective of the philosophic posture (value system) of the person observing and talking.

3. The interplay of these three variables (perception, language, and value system) influences the nature of the teaching-learning experience (communication).

7

4. The language of a profession can a priori determine perceptions and consequently human experience.

Perceptions, Language, and Values

Bloom (1978) argues that in order to improve the schooling experience, educators must remove from their minds certain constructs relative to their perceptions of children. When teachers are asked to picture and describe a "good student," without exception the description falls within the range of the two constructs of intelligence and behavior. Educational decisions are made and instructional experiences determined on the basis of whether students are smart or dumb, fast or slow, and good or ornery. The education profession could not have been less imaginative.

As a consequence of these constructs with their inherently limited vision, there have evolved essentially three sets of metaphors used in talking about children; (a) military, (b) industrial, and (c) disease. These metaphors and their relationship to research on teacher effectiveness and efficiency are discussed in Chapter 4. Examples of the language associated with each of these three metaphors are:

Military Metaphor - target population, information systems, centralization of power, line and staff, scheduling, discipline, govern, maintain, objectives, strategy, training, firing line, in-the-trenches.

Industrial Metaphor - management, cost effectiveness, efficiency, institutional planning, programming, output measure, product, feedback, defective, input-process-output, quality control.

Disease Metaphor - diagnostic, prescription, treatment, remediation, monitor, label, deviant, impaired, referral procedure, special needs.

Heubner (1963) classifies values into five frameworks: (a) technical, (b) political, (c) scientific, (d) aesthetic, and (e) ethical. Technical values have resulted in an ideology almost totally concerned with activities producing defined ends, ususally in the form of predetermined behavior. Political values tend to promote the idea of a person's worth being judged by his/her influence. Power and control become the end. Scientific values promote activities which produce new knowledge with an empirical base. Aesthetic values tend to generate activities which can be felt and lived by children. Ethical values promote the idea that educational activities are life and that life's meanings are witnessed and lived in the classroom. None of these value systems is inherently destructive; however, the exaggerated dependence on some to the exclusion of others is dangerous. Current educational ideology reflects almost completely technical and political value systems. In summary, educators use essentially two constructs, three metaphors, and five value systems when looking at, talking about, and living with children.

An Alternative

We are suggesting the need for alternative constructs and language for viewing and talking about children in order to enhance their educational living experiences. We believe new constructs and language can be derived from aesthetic and ethical value systems. Other sources in the literature (Berman, 1968; Dobson & Dobson, 1976, 1981; Eisner, 1979; Leonard, 1972; Macdonald, 1968) support this view.

Aesthetic and Ethical Viewing

Rogers' (1951) theoretical formulations of his theory of personality and behavior can be used (in part) as a conceptual framework for viewing children from an aesthetic and ethical value base. Central to looking at children is the premise that "the best vantage point for understanding behavior is from the internal frame of reference of the individual himself" (p. 494). Too often, teachers observe children's behaviors and evaluate them from an external frame of reference. When viewing children's behaviors, teachers must be cognizant of the premise (Rogers, 1951) that behavior is goal directed and is based upon the private world of children, their realities. Granted, children's goals and their realities may be only partially in their consciousness; not completely in children's awareness. There is, however, the potential for children to become aware of and understand their personal goals and realities. The teacher, on the other hand, will never completely understand the private world of children. Rogers (1951) continues, "...no matter how much we attempt to measure the perceiving organism--whether by psychometric tests or physiological calibration--it is still true that the individual is the only one who can know how the experience was perceived" (p. 484).

The importance of self-concept is stressed by Rogers (1951, p. 507) when he states, "Most of the ways of behaving which are adopted by the organism are those which are consistent with the concept of self." The child who perceives self as inadequate academically, socially, or personally will generally behave in such a manner at school, as does the child who perceives self as adequate in these areas. Purkey (1978, p. 30) states, "...one's self-concept is a complex, continuously active system of subjective beliefs about one's personal existence." The self-concept serves as a guide or a reference point for one's behavior (Glock, 1972). What children experience is filtered through and mediated by their concepts of self, images they have learned from significant others over the years. Since the self-concept serves as a mediator of perceptions, thoughts, and actions, then the images children hold of themselves are of utmost importance.

Aesthetic and Ethical Language

Macdonald (1968) opens the way for ethical talk by suggesting that curriculum should be assessed with moral constructs which can be extended to view the instructional act as well. Among his suggested moral constructs are dialogue, promise, forgiveness, service, justice, beauty, and vitality.

Creating an instructional experience sensitive to open communication requires educators to take into consideration the notion of dialogue, a process which implies that what everyone has to say carries equal weight. This does not mean that children have all the decision-making power, but rather that what children have to say is important and must be seriously considered. The implication of dialogue within the educational setting has been established by Freire (1970) and Koetting (1980).

Teachers' promise that educational experiences will have personal meaning for learners is a basic human learning right. Teachers must be secure enough to promise caring and to follow through on the process of meeting the personal, psychological, social, and emotional needs of children.

Risk-taking is necessary in learning and growth. School environments functioning solely from the right-wrong answer and appropriate behavior syndromes might entertain the alternative of "goofing up." There is a vast difference between "goofing up" and being wrong. Forgiveness becomes a necessary variable in such an environment.

One major purpose of schooling is to foster the unlimited potential of the child to love, to learn, to create, and to grow. If educators accept this basic premise, then one function of the school is to provide service to the participants. Decisions and activities are geared toward providing service; administrative convenience and teaching comfort become secondary in importance.

Judgment without justice is an inhumane activity degrading the dignity and worth of the individual. Rules or guidelines are a necessary part of a smooth functioning school and are created to help, rather than hinder individuals. When rules cease to fulfill this obligation they should be eliminated. To establish a single rule taking into consideration all the complex variables associated with a given situation would be a horrendous, if not an impossible, task. Each situation has its own elements of justice and its own rules. Rules must be used only when they facilitate an individual's development.

The concept of beauty relates to children's potentials to extend, create, and grow through personal meaning, not in being judged on outcomes determined and desired by others. When children become mere objects or pawns of their school environments, the vehicle for extension and realization of beauty is subjugated.

All of these previously mentioned constructs--dialogue, promise, forgiveness, service, justice, and beauty--are dependent upon the moral constructs of vitality, emancipation and praxis; that is, as inhabitants within schools gain new understandings, they must be willing to change the existing structures of the schools.

Aesthetic and Ethical Living Experiences

The focal point of the school experience is the person, and what happens or does not happen to the person is a matter of aesthetic and ethical consideration. Teaching is, first and foremost, a moral enterprise because educators intervene in people's lives. What educators decide to do to, for, or with children is value based and of primary importance. Macdonald (1968, p. 38) illuminates the significance of the person when he states "...a person has worth not because of his unique individuality but primarily because he is a person." He continues, "A person is not to be thought of as a bundle of needs, or interests, or unique purposes that can be directed or guided or developed to someone's statisfaction" (p. 30).

In considering the value base of the relationship of persons in a classroom setting, Frymier (1972, p. 13) suggests "...there are languages of conditional relationships and the relationships without conditions: the first is a language of 'control'; the second is a language of 'love and growth'."

The language of the technical model applied to the classroom experience suggests scientific accuracy and predictability (scientific values) and the nature of this model has an interest in control (political values). The historical roots of these orientations have been outlined by others (Apple, 1979; Giroux, 1980; Kliebard, 1975). Tabachnick, Popkowitz, and Zeichner (1979-80), in their research on the student teaching experience, observed that students were engaged in the "routine and mechanistic teaching of precise and short-term skills and in management activities designed to keep the class quiet, orderly, and on task" (p. 16).

Dobson, Dobson, and Koetting (1982) state the language of the technical model applied to teaching effectiveness research has contributed to simplistic, input/output understandings of educational experiences ("student-as-product" orientation). The technical model, along with the language of technical-rationale, suggests that the "right mix" of technique and content will significantly increase student performance. Teaching is viewed as a "science and technology" with identifiable skills lending themselves to short-term teaching goals which focus on a utilitarian perspective. Tabachnick, et al. (1979-80) suggest that this view leads to a managerial understanding of teaching.

11

A case has been established that aesthetic and ethical considerations have been slighted, if not totally ignored, in the creation of living experiences occuring in classroom settings. In light of this condition, Greene (1973, p. 6) suggests if teachers want to be themselves and achieve something meaningful in the world they should subscribe to a proposal "...which is nothing more than to think what we are doing."

The method we propose for beginning the search for conditions reflecting aesthetic and ethical values in the classroom setting is the awakening of consciousness through dialogue. According to Freire (1981), an educational experience placing dialogue at its center starts the dialogical process. "It is a questioning process about possible 'thematic universes' expressing the relationships of the persons involved in dialogue with the world" (Freire, 1981, p. 86).

A dialogical situation serves the purpose of clarifying the teacher's and learner's thoughts with one another. In this process, students no longer learn in isolation, but rather in world context with one another. This process involves not only the cognition of a given situation, but also a reconsideration of personal ways of approaching the situation under study. When teachers and students reflect on their being through the building of new structures of meanings they become aware they are building themselves in the process. For Pritzkau (1970) dialogue is, "...conversation between two or more persons in which each transcends his solitude and accepts his aloneness and that of the other person, thereby seeking a form of transaction which maintains the maximum freedom of each" (pp. 11-12).

Dialogue for Freire (1981) corresponds to a dual process of denunciation and annunciation. He expresses:

Our pedagogy cannot do without a vision of man and the world. It formulates scientific humanist conception which finds its expression in a dialogical praxis in which the teachers and learners together, in the act of analyzing a dehumanizing reality, denounce it while announcing its transformation in the name of the liberation of man. (p. 338)

Denunciation and annunciation are both hope and action. Hope is the belief of one's inner capability to become whomever one decides to be, guided by value considerations. Action is the actualization of one's hope, one's intent to direct the course of his/her life through the use of human freedom.

It is immoral to expect teachers and learners to continue leaving their "persons" outside the door as they enter the classroom. Teachers and learners need not be expected to assume postures of value neutrality as they don the masks of their assigned roles. Dialogical praxis is a process for dealing with human qualities (internal manifestations of beliefs and values) which people bring to the arena of human interaction.

Conclusion

Edelman (1973) suggests that language used by educators tends to establish their reality and subtly justify their actions. This function is not unique to any one philosophic position. Well-intended proponents of differing positions sometimes are more concerned with rhetoric than with what is best for children and society. We suggest responsible educators spend time and effort in examining the value base(s) of their perceptions and the professional language used in "looking at and talking about" children. Only then will the roots of their philosophic stances be uncovered which influcence the kinds of living experiences provided children. In Chapter 2 we offer one interpretative view of the schooling experience which expands on the ideas presented in this chapter.

References

Appignanesi, R. (1976). Finding one's own voice. In A. Wesker, Words as definition of experience (pp. 19-43). Great Britain: Writers & Publishers' Corporation.

Apple M. (1975a). Scientific interests and the nature of educational institutions. In W. Pinar (Ed.), Curriculum theorizing: The reconceptualists (pp. 120-130). Berkeley: McCutchan.

Apple, M. (1975b). Commonsense categories and curriculum thought. In J. Macdonald & E. Zaret (Eds.), Schools in search of meaning (pp. 116-148). Washington, DC: Association of Supervision and Curriculum Development.

Apple, M. (1979). Ideology and curriculum. London: Routledge & Kegan Paul, Ltd.

Berman, L. (1968). New priorities in the curriculum. Columbus, OH: Charles E. Merrill.

Bloom, B. (1978). New views of the learner: Implications for instruction and curriculum. Educational Leadership, 35, 558-561.

Dobson, R. L., & Dobson, J. E. (1976). Humaneness in schools: A neglected force. Dubuque, IA: Kendall/Hunt.

Dobson, R. L., & Dobson, J. E. (1981). The Language of schooling. Washington, DC: University Press of America.

Dobson, R. L., Dobson, J. E. & Koetting, J. R. (1982, Spring). The language of teaching-effectiveness and teacher competency research. Viewpoints in teaching and learning, 58 (2), 23-33.

Edelman, M. (1973). The political language of the helping professions. Unpublished manuscript, University of Wisconsin, Madison.

Eisner, E. (1979) The educational imagination. New York: Macmillian.

Freire, P. (1970). Pedagogy of the oppressed. New York: Seabury Press.

Freire, P. (1981). The adult literacy process as cultural action for freedom. In J. R. Snarey, F. Epstein, C. Sienkiewicz, & P. Zodhiates (Eds.), Conflict and continuity: A history of ideas on social equality and human development (pp. 87-115). (Reprint Series No. 15). Boston: Harvard Educational Review.

Frymier, J. R. (1972). A curriculum manifesto. Oceanside, OR: Curriculum Bulletin.

14

Giroux, H. A. (1980). Teacher education and the ideology of social control. Journal of Education, 162(1), 5-27.

Glock, M. (1972). Is there a pygmalion in the classroom? The Reading Teacher, 25(5), 405-409.

Greene, M. (1973). Teacher as stanger. Belmont, CA: Wadsworth.

Habermas, J. (1971). Knowledge and human interests. Boston: Beacon Press.

Huebner, D. (1966). Curriculum language and classroom meanings. In J. Macdonald & R. Leeper (Eds.), Language and meaning (pp. 8-26). Washington, DC: Association for Supervision and Curriculum Development.

Kliebard, H. (1975). Bureaucracy and curriculum theory. In W. Pinar (Ed.), Curriculum theorizing: The reconceptualists (pp. 51-69). Berkeley: McCutchan.

Koetting, J. R. (1980). Towards a synthesis of a theory of knowledge and human interests, educational technology and emancipatory education: A preliminary theoretical investigation and critique. (Doctoral Dissertation, University of Wisconsin-Madison, 1979). Dissertation Abstracts International, 40, 6118A.

Leonard, G. (1972). The transformation. New York: Delacorte.

Macdonald, J. (1968). A curriculum rationale. In E. Short & G. Marconnit (Eds.), Contempory thoughts on public school curriculum (pp. 37-41). Dubuque, IA: William C. Brown.

Pritzkau, P. F. (1970). On education for the authentic. New York: Thomas J. Crowell.

Purkey, W. (1978). Inviting school success. Belmont, CA: Wadsworth.

Rogers, C. R. (1951). Client-centered therapy. Boston: Houghton Mifflin.

Tabachnick, R., Popkowitz, S., & Zeichner, K. M. (1979-80). Teacher education and the professional perspectives of student teachers. Interchange, 10, 12-29.

Tranel, D. (1981). A lesson from physicists. Personnel and Guidance Journal, 59, 425-429.

Wesker, A. (1976). Words as definitions of experience. Great Britain: Writers & Publishers Cooperative.

Wickman, E. (1929). <u>Children's behavior and teachers' attitudes.</u> New York: Commonwealth Fund Division of Publications.

The first chapter identified our value-stance which is
evident throughout the subsequent chapters: Educators need
to reflect upon their own value base(s) in their perceptions of
children and the professional language they use in looking at
and talking about children. This could be an emancipatory,
reflective activity wherein the philosophical base of schooling
providing the rationale for living experiences with children
may be consciously discovered and result in an informed
praxis. In Chapter 2 we offer an interpretative view of the
schooling experience. It is our contention that the absence of
reflective activity concerning the philosophical bases and
values held by educators has contributed to a phenomenon in
the schools that we refer to as "cloning."

We argue that the dominant view of schooling today has
as one of its major functions the psychological and
sociological "cloning" of its clientele. We further argue that
this function is fulfilled through the hidden curriculum. We
identify major "cloning strategies" practiced by schools and
the sources of self-validation through cloning offered by
schools.

CHAPTER 2

THE CLONING OF AMERICA*

In 1970 Charles Reich published a book titled The Greening of America, reflecting the pulse of the educational community's concern for the freedom of all children to reach toward their unlimited potential to love, create, learn, and grow. A decade later, for a variety of reasons, it appears significant numbers of the profession have become almost pathologically preoccupied with an antithetical pastime, "the cloning of America." Cloning, a biological term, is defined as asexual reproduction which results in exact genetic duplicates of the original. We submit that current trends in the schooling experience, either by intent or accident, are subtly encouraging the psychological and sociological cloning of children.

The cloning syndrome is directly related to the concept of the "one model American." While the American school system purports to prize diversity and honor human variability, many educators are engaged in activities that seek to homogenize. The notion of "one model American" simply does not match the tenets of our society, with its multivalue base reflecting cultural pluralism. A monolithic public school system cannot support the diversity inherent in and demanded by a democracy. In Chapter I an argument was made that viewing and talking about children from a pseudo-scientific (strict objectivity) frame of reference has encouraged the entrenchment of a technocratic-rationale in the research and design of school experiences for children. This chapter expands this point by discussing the major cloning tools and sources of personal validation present in American schools. We believe educators have created a farce by assuming that the end result of the public schooling experience should be a product, a youth who is a carbon copy of peers. We also believe the "deficit model" that has become the strategy for educational planning and design is a direct reflection of the "cloning syndrome" which has infiltrated educational practices.

Cloning Tools

The psychological and sociological tools of cloning, although somewhat deceptive, are present and in use in today's schools and fulfilled through the hidden curriculum. Prevalent among these tools are (a) diagnosis with concommitant emphasis on testing, (b) labeling and stereotyping, (c) ability grouping, and (d) positive reinforcement.

Diagnosis. Generally speaking, standardized testing in schools has a tendency to penalize students for what they do not know as opposed to rewarding them for what they do know. Possibly, educators'

---

*This chapter is a revised version of our article which first appeared in The School Counselor, 29 (1) (Sept., 1981), 13-21. Copyright 1981 TSC.

19

preoccupation with those things which can be measured has caused them to lose sight of those things that "should" be measured. Seemingly, educators have developed a fetish for those aspects of human nature that lend themselves to symbols. To assume that one can begin to determine or entertain all the complexities associated with a human being is probably ridiculous. The inadequacies of educators in this respect have resulted in negative perceptions and uses of testing. If educators can determine a deficiency through testing, then they also should be able to prescribe and remediate. The result is the correction syndrome. As Weller (1977, p. 6) so succintly states: "Man has come to be seen as the sum total of his ills, problems, and deficiencies. It is as if a person to be educated can be equated with a problem to be solved."

We do not deny that youngsters need and desire feedback about their growth and development. However, we believe this need should be met when an invitation is extended by the child and by focusing on strengths and successes.

Labeling. Labeling is a process whereby one human agent or group makes a value judgement about the appropriateness or inappropriateness of another's actions, thoughts, or being.

Clinical terms used to label children in schools tend to function as a form of social control; that is, the sorting of children into preordained social, economic, and educational slots (Apple, 1975). Labels serve as distancing factors (Buscaglia, 1972) between students and teachers, allowing for the treatment of students as objects as opposed to viewing them as persons. Furthermore, people tend to live up to the labels assigned to them. Rosenthal (1970) and Silberman (1970) suggest society has assigned teachers the role of "Gatekeepers" of society whose function is to select winners and losers.

Labeling is one of education's greatest industries. Once a professional is trained in labeling, it becomes necessary to find or create individuals to fit those labels in order to maintain employment. When this effort is exhausted it becomes necessary to create new labels for yet-to-be-discovered clients. While this action is occuring, two myths are in operation: (a) If an individual is experiencing a problem then the fault lies with the individual and not the institution; and (b) All people who possess the characteristics inherent to a particular label are the same and treatment should be similar.

Ability Grouping. Homogeneous grouping is a practice whereby the total student body is divided into instructional groups according to some criterion of likeness. The basic premise for ability grouping is the belief that learning is facilitated when children of similar potential, ability, or academic achievement are placed together for instruction. This type of classroom organization appears to lessen slightly the range of abilities within a group.

20

Advocates of homogeneous groupings are vociferous in expounding the merits of this arrangement. The proclaimed strengths are: (a) Special attention can be given to childrens' abilities or talents; (b) Superior academic achievement is obtained; (c) Materials and procedures can easily be adapted; and (d) This method is logical and easy to administer. No evidence supports these claims made by advocates of ability grouping. In cases where research evidence seems to point to achievement gains in favor of homogeneous grouping, the same gains can be attributed to the accompanying variables of teaching method, materials, resources, or curriculum reorganization.

What does exist is evidence to suggest homogeneous grouping has detrimental effects on the academic and social growth of children (Borg, 1966; Deutsch, 1963; Dockrell, 1975; Esposito, 1973; Heather, 1964; Johnson & Johnson, 1975; Purdom, 1929; Rosenthal & Jacobson, 1968; Squire, 1966). A now classic study by Daniels (1961) established that only 2% of the students once assigned to an ability group are ever shifted.

A disproportionate number of children from low income homes are assigned to low ability groups. Contrary to popular belief, this assigning is done on the basis of reading scores as opposed to scores on intelligence tests (Wechsler, 1974). Ability grouping can thus be viewed as a tool for maintaining caste and class stratification in society. One can argue, therefore, that in homogenous grouping (a) children are typed and placed at one level permanently, (b) children are segregated, a situation inconsistent with democratic values, (c) teachers are encouraged to believe children placed in one group are alike, and (d) peer stimulation created by various abilities and talents is lacking.

Positive reinforcement. Many educators seem to believe that adults, because of their experiences, know what children should be when they grow up, and it is the school's responsibility to assist children in conforming to this model of adulthood (Dobson & Dobson, 1975). This thinking is evidenced by the current interest in techniques for controlling and directing behavior through positive and negative reinforcement. Motivation has come to be seen as a way of getting children to do and learn what others want them to do and learn. It is as if some educators have a fetish for gold stars, dunce caps, and crushed bananas.

In 1976, Dobson and Dobson wrote:

To deny that positive reinforcement is more satisfying than negative reinforcement would be stupid; however, educators must recognize that both are externally directed. There is the ever present danger that over a period of time children will reach the point where they perform only when an incentive is available. If educators are committed to the notion of the self-directed learner, then placing an excessive amount of value on behavior modification techniques may delay unnecessarily, if not permanently, the learner's acceptance of

21

responsibility for his own learning. There is much to be said for pure ecstacy or joy which is a self reward of learning. If learning is viewed as a rational, evolving phenomenon then educators may not be so eager to interfere with youngsters' growth. It can be argued that if young children are constantly subjected to manipulation, reward-punishment systems, they could be limited or crippled intellectually and emotionally, resulting in limited human potential and thus condemned to a life of immaturity. Necessary intervention in a child's life is one thing, arrogant interference is quite another. Current behavior modification techniques are teacher-initiated and used primarily for controlling children, not for facilitating learning. (pp. 23-24)

Throughout the years our thoughts relative to this statement have intensified. A series of experiments (Deci, 1972a, 1972b; Garbarino, 1975; Lepper & Greene, 1976) provide evidence supporting the proposition that extrinsic rewards subsequently impair an individual's access to intrinsic motivation and in some instances even have detrimental effects.

Validation by Cloning

We believe that an important function of "growing up" is to validate self, to establish one's position relative to time, circumstance, and place. To establish one's position as worthy, to view one's posture as both participatory and contributing to the environment, requires opportunities to experience liking and being liked, success, involvement, and acceptance. Self-validation is the opposite of validation by cloning.

The sources of validation by cloning provided by the schooling experience more often than not serve as dehumanizing experiences for some of our young. Among sources of validation by cloning provided by schools are (a) correct behavior, (b) grades, (c) performance, (d) honors and awards, and (e) parental status. These sources affect, and in some instances determine, the student's appraisal of self and of the world in general.

Correct Behavior. Educators seem to prefer conforming behavior over divergent and nonconforming behavior within the school setting. All too often, children are taught to perceive in a certain way, not necessarily their individual ways. The child is made to believe that the teacher, being the individual with authority, perceives correctly as a matter of course. This process "...begins at an early age and gradually through repetitive conditioning and reward or fear of punishment and rejection..." (Moustakas, 1967, p. 87) children begin to act in fairly standard ways. The result of this tradition-bound standard of behavior dictated in schools is often conformity or rebellion by children.

Conforming children do not use their own experiences but take their directions from outside sources, persons in authority. These children have

22

given up their actual identities and assumed acceptable group modes of thinking and doing. Moustakas (1967) eloquently states the results of conformity:

> When a person's involvement in a situation is based on appearances, expectations, or the standards of others; when he acts in a conventional manner, or according to prescribed roles and functions; when he is concerned with status and approval; his growth as a creative self is impaired. When the individual is conforming, following, imitating, being like others, he moves increasingly in the direction of self-alienation. (p. 35)

Instead of conformity, some youngsters choose to rebel against the school's standards of behavior. These youngsters are well known to counselors, teachers, and principals and often are labeled as troublemakers, truants, underachievers, and nonconformists.

Grading. Grades also are a source of validation by cloning, the reward and punishment characteristic of our tradition-bound educational system. We wonder how often teachers threaten students with: "If you don't hand in your work you'll flunk second grade or ...seventh grade or ...you'll not be accepted into college ...or get a job." We also wonder how teachers can possibly assess learning for all students by using only five letters of the alphabet. Postman and Weingartner (1971, p. 113) state "...that the purpose of an education has nothing to do with grades, and that grades tend to pollute the learning environment."

Dreikurs, Grunwald and Pepper (1971) contend that motivated students who are or can be stimulated to learn without grades are the only students who respond to grading. The less motivated students tend to shrug them off as continual proof of their inadequacies. Therefore, they state that grades "...are neither needed nor effective" (p. 179).

The current marking system, identifying wrong answers, cannot be logically defended by teachers, administrators, students, or parents who agree that the primary purpose of formal education is to encourage life-long learning and development. Dreikurs et al. (1971) recommend providing feedback to students concerning their learning and that this be a cooperative endeavor involving the teacher and the student. They also recommend parent-teacher conferences be substituted for the traditional report card so that parents and teachers alike gain a deeper appreciation for the child's personal, social, and academic growth. Glasser (1969, p. 95) suggests "...that no student ever at any time be labeled a failure through the use of the grading system." This suggestion is based upon the belief that grades emphasize failure more than success and that failure is the basis of most school problems.

Performance. Teachers are constantly making judgements concerning student performance. School performance, however, generally refers to the acquisition of subject matter content. Teachers are often

23

asked, "Is the student performing at grade level?" The very nature of this question suggests a source of cloning, comparing a child to others approximately the same chronological age. Why is it educators accept that children about the same age differ physically (simple observation proves this) but will not entertain the notion of differences in the rate of academic, personal, and social development? All too often, children who do not meet grade level expectations are considered school failures and labeled as slow learners, non-readers, under-achievers, or learning disabled.

Leonard (1968) alludes to educators' attempts to clone when he states:

Indeed, the entire education process as it is usually constituted in our schools may best be viewed as a funnel through which every child is squeezed into an ever-narrowing circle....(p. 112)

Performance in school settings often refers to the score obtained on an objective test. The emphasis is on the correct answer. Glasser (1969, p. 69) states, "...objective testing is the landmark of fact-centered education." He comments that instead of using objective tests, teachers must encourage students to broaden their outlooks, to explore the uncertain, the unknown.

Standardized tests have been criticized and defended (Redman, 1977) and minimal competency testing is making the news (Pipho, 1978). Goodlad (1979, p. 343) suggests, "...the norm by which the performance of schools is now judged is entirely inadequate, from one perspective, and, from another corrupts the educative process." He continues that if education is to be judged by student performance then the appraisal of performance must be broadened to include social and personal skills and knowledge as well as academic content.

Honors and Awards. Recognition or acknowledgement by others of a job well done can be a very satisfactory experience for most people, young and old alike. Many people, however, seem to thrive solely upon the honors and awards given by others, and the schools seem to perpetuate the "doing in order to receive awards" philosophy.

Who receives honors or awards in school? Generally, those who receive institutional recognition are those who are willing to work within the system. Accolades are given to those students, teachers, principals, and superintendents who do what they are told, when they are told to do so. Therefore, honors and awards are given for doing appropriate things at appropriate times. The concept of "appropriateness" is arbitrarily determined by external forces.

Children learn early the critera necessary for achieving honors and awards. How sad that in our society these criteria are available on a

24

disproportionate basis and are largely unavailable to children of low socioeconomic status and non-Caucasian people.

Parental Status. Another source of validation by cloning is the emphasis placed upon the status one's parents have within the community. Have you attended a school program lately? More often than not, the students who had the lead roles in the production have parents who are well known in the community. Similarly, while attending a high school sporting event, notice the names of the cheerleaders. Once again, the majority of the young people selected for the cheerleading squad are those whose parents have some status within the community. From these two simple observations, one may conclude that in many schools today, those students who are "in," so to speak, are those who feel secure enough to risk trying out for various performances and groups, and are ones whose parents have obtained some status within the community.

This has not changed since Packard (1959, p. 11) succinctly stated, "...the car you drive, the church you attend...the house you live in...is your status--and you may be stuck with it, like it or not." Evidently, most of our schools have become the preservers of middle-class values, aspirations, and traditions by continually validating those students who come from certain neighborhoods or whose parents hold prestigious jobs or own a successful business.

If schools are truly to educate all children and youth in our pluralistic society, then educators must find ways to enlist the involvement and support of parents from all ethnic and economic levels of the community. Dobson and Dobson (1975) suggest parental participation in the school experience can integrate children's school and home lives and provide them with a mode of participation and control in a major area of life. Certainly validation of self through parental status must be questioned and give way to active participation of students and parents from all community subcultures and socioeconomic levels.

A Concluding Statement

When school sources of validation are not open to all young people, they may pursue other means which are accessible. The media has overwhelmed us with information about these avenues which can, in many cases, be appropriately termed escape avenues. Examples of these are high school dropout, drug culture, cultism, and violence. We could add to this list. As responsible adults, educators must question the quality of these alternatives for self-validation of our young. Perhaps our mission as educators is two-fold in nature: (a) We must seek to improve the educational structure; and (b) We must ensure that all young people have equal opportunity to take advantage of the sources available for developing their uniqueness.

Our intent in writing this chapter has not been to launch an attack on the U.S. school system. Rather, our intent is to submit the idea of

25

cloning to a community of experts (teachers, counselors, and administrators) for consideration and contemplation. The time has come for theorists and practitioners to come to grips with a re-evaluation of their educational platforms. The issues of perception, language, practice, and behavior engineering, identified in Chapters 1 and 2, must be faced: Do we shape children into what they should be or do we nurture their growth toward what they may be? A question of this nature does not lend itself to simplistic answers.

References

Apple, M. (1975). Commonsense categories and curriculum thought. In J. Macdonald & E. Zaret (Eds.), Schools in search of meaning (pp. 116-150). Washington, DC: Association for Supervision and Curriculum Development.

Borg, W. R. (1966). Ability grouping in the public schools (2nd ed.). Madison, WI: Dembar Educational Research Services.

Buscaglia, L. F. (1972). Love. Thoroughfare, NJ: Charles B. Slack.

Daniels, J. C. (1961). Effects of streaming in the primary school: A comparison of streamed and unstreamed schools. British Journal of Educational Psychology, 31, 119-27.

Deci, E. L. (1972a). Changes in intrinsic motivation as a function of negative feedback and threats. Rochester, NY: Rochester University. (ERIC Document Reproduction Service No. ED 063 558)

Deci, E. L. (1972b). Intrinsic motivation, extrinsic reinforcement and inequity. Journal of Personality and Social Psychology, 22, 113-129.

Deutsch, M A. (1963). Dimensions in the school's role in problems of integration. In G. Klopf & I. Loster (Eds.), Integration in the urban school (pp. 114-147). New York: Teachers College, Columbia University.

Dobson, R. L., & Dobson, J. E. (1975) Parental and community involvement in education and teacher education. Washington, DC: ERIC Clearinghouse on Teacher Education. (ERIC Document Reproduction Service No. SP 008 742)

Dobson, R. L., & Dobson, J. E. (1976). Humaneness in schools: A neglected force. Dubuque, IA: Kendall/Hunt.

Dockrell, W. B. (1975). Edmonton junior high school streaming project. Studies in grouping. Toronto, Canada: Alberta Teacher's Association.

Dreikurs, R., Grunwald, B., & Pepper, F. C. (1971). Maintaining sanity in the classroom: Illustrated teaching techniques. New York: Harper & Row.

Esposito, D. (1973). Homogenous and heterogenous ability grouping: Principal findings and implications for evaluating and designing more effective educational environments. Review of Educational Research, 33, 163-79.

Garbarino, J. (1975). The impact of anticipated reward upon cross-age tutoring. Journal of Personality and Social Psychology, 32, 421-28.

Glasser, W. (1969). Schools without failure. New York: Harper & Row.

Goodlad, J. (1979). Can our schools get better? Phi Delta Kappan, 5, 342-47.

Heather, G. (1964). Research on team teaching. In S. A. Sharlin & W. B. Olds (Eds.), Team Teaching (pp. 120-137). New York: Harper & Row.

Johnson, P., & Johnson, R. (1975). Learning together and alone: Cooperation, competition, and individualization. Englewood Cliffs, NJ: Prentice Hall.

Lepper, M. R., & Greene, D. (1976). On understanding 'overjustification': A reply to Reiss and Suskinsky. Journal of Personality and Social Psychology, 33, 25-35.

Leonard, G. (1968). Education and ecstacy. New York: Delacorte.

Moustakas, C. E. (1967). Creativity and conformity. Princeton, NJ: D. Van Norstrand.

Packard, V. (1959). The status seekers. New York: Pocket Books.

Pipho, C. (Ed.). (1978). Minimal competency testing. Phi Delta Kappan, 59, 585-625.

Postman, N., & Weingartner, C. (1971). The soft revolution. New York: Dell.

Purdom, L. T. (1929). The value of homogenous grouping. York, PA: Maple Press.

Redman, H. C. (1977). The standardized test flap. Phi Delta Kappan, 59, 179-85.

Reich, C. (1970). The greening of America. New York: Random House.

Rosenthal, R. (1970). Teacher expectation and pupil learning. In N. Overly (Ed.), The unstudied curriculum (pp. 53-84). Washington, DC: Association for Supervision and Curriculum Development.

Rosenthal, R., & Jacobson, L. (1968). Pygmalion in the classroom: Teacher expectations and pupils' intellectual development. New York: Holt, Rinehart & Winston.

Silberman, C. E. (1970). Crisis in the classroom. New York: Random House.

Squire, J. P. (1966). National study of high school English programs: A school for all seasons. English Journal, 55, 282-90.

Wechsler, D. (1974). Selected papers of David Wechsler. New York: Academic Press.

Weller, R. H. (Ed.). (1977). Humanistic education. Berkeley: McCutchan.

SECTION II

STATE OF THE ART: DIVERGENT VIEWS

Arriving at consensus relative to the purposes and functions of schooling requires responses to complex questions for which there are probably no "best" answers. Expressed purposes of schooling are as diversified and unique as the individual perceptual filters of those providing opinions.

Indeed, if we are to pursue the roots of reality relative to the purpose of schooling, we must uncover the meanings of words blurred by custom and usage. The crucial need is for "languaging"--a way of discussing issues without arguing. Certainly, in a democracy with a pluralistic or multi-value base, there is need for a communication vehicle which will assist people to approach consensus concerning the schooling of the young. Responsible educators cannot afford to leave the education of the young to the persuasive powers of a few.

Advocates of various curriculum camps identified in Chapter 3 use language in an attempt to homogenize social reality. The use of language to establish reality and subtly justify actions is not a function unique to any one philosophic camp.

At times it appears that well-intentioned proponents of differing philosophic postures are more concerned with political rhetoric than with what is best and decent for children and the larger society. We would recommend an attempt at dialogical praxis as a worthy activity for the vocal proponents of the diverse camps. This seems to be a good beginning for providing the young with an intellectually honest and decent schooling experience.

It seems safe to assume that proponents of various philosophic camps are more concerned with finding better ways of doing what they are already doing than with raising questions as to why they do what they do. Curriculum and pedagogical issues are a consequence of diverse conceptualizations of reality and values. Section II enables persons interested in the purposes and functions of schooling to make useful distinctions among three explicit curriculum camps.

In Chapter 2 we argued that the dominant view of schooling today has as one of its major functions the psychological and sociological "cloning" of its clientele. In Chapter 3 we continue to examine the language educators use in looking at and talking about children. This is done through the presentation of a model for schooling dialogue which can be used to critique three philosophical schools of thought.

CHAPTER 3

THE LANGUAGE OF SCHOOLING*

Two thousand years ago the Stoic philosopher Epictetus wrote, "Men are disturbed not by things, but by the vision which they take of them." Being critical of the nation's schools has moved from hobby stage to a full-blown national sport. One can scarcely read a daily newspaper, current magazine, or educational journal without finding an article criticizing some aspect of public schools.

Some educators have a tendency to be pragmatic and react to pressures: They seem to be more interested in methods and programs than in theories. With only a superficial understanding of the basic theories on which curriculum decisions are based, educators often implement unwisely, and when techniques do not yield expected results or come under criticism from pressure groups, ideas and programs are rejected as hastily as they were accepted. We believe if educators do not understand why they do what they do, then they do it poorly.

In any event, in a time when educators are continuously concerned with finding better ways of doing what they are already doing, and citizens are eager to hold them accountable, is it not time to reassess the purposes of schooling, if indeed such purposes can be identified? Ebel (1972) states:

> We seem to have lost sight of, or become confused about, our main function as educators, our principal goal, our reason for existence. We have no good answer that we are sure of and can agree on to the question, What are schools for? (p. 3)

Deciding on the purposes of schooling requires responses to complex questions for which there are probably no best answers. Some argue that the critical philosophic issue in education is freedom. This may be so. If it is, then there is a crucial need for "languaging"--a way of talking without shouting. The Spanish philosopher Jose Ortega y Gassett (1967) establishes:

> The words of a language have their meaning imposed by collective usage. Speaking is a re-using of that accepted meaning, saying what is already known, what everyone knows, what is mutually known. (p. 60)

However, the question remains: Do words, or for that matter the lack of words, control thoughts or do words express thoughts? If we are to pursue

---

*This chapter is an edited version of our article which first appeared under the title "Model for Curriculum Dialogue" in Forum on Open Education, 4, (5) (February, 1977), 3-13. Copyright 1977 FOE.

the roots of reality relative to the purposes of schooling, we must uncover meanings blurred by custom and usage. "This will require 'revivifying' or 'resucitating' the meanings" (Frazier, 1970, p. 28).

Certainly, in a democracy with a pluralistic or multi-value base, there is need for a communication vehicle assisting individuals as well as the public in approaching consensus concerning the schooling of the young. Responsible educators cannot afford to leave the education of the young to the persuasive powers of a few.

An anonymous sage once said, "The cause of anything is everything." This assumption embodies the notion of the interrelatedness of all things. Today the search goes on for the purposes of schooling. The purposes, no doubt, are varied and interrelated and result from attempts to answer two historical questions asked by Macdonald (1977): (a) What is the meaning of life? and (b) How can we work together?

From a historical perspective it is no surprise that in a troubled society some will seek national solutions through the schools. Let us recapitulate. There is a progressively widening split in the ranks of people concerned with purposes of the school experience. This split has resulted in definite trends in both theory and practice.

As schools constantly entertain pressure and attempt to constructively interact with critics, it would be useful to have a classification tool for categorizing varying opinions about schooling. Table I titled, The Language of Schooling, is presented as such a device. We share this model dialectically. The content of the model is presented for contemplation and discussion purposes only and is not intended to be final in nature.

Table I is an attempt to identify and contrast three philosophical and psychological profiles tending to separate into three camps: (a) Design A, (b) Design B, and (c) Design C. This separation is quite possibly a direct reflection of whether persons are primarily concerned with doing to, for, or with young people. The three camps can be dispersed on a continuum ranging from training to education.*

Training (To)	(For)	Education (With)
$\longleftarrow$		$\longrightarrow$
(Essentialism- Behaviorism)	(Experimentalism- Cognition)	(Existentialism- Humanism)

*For a more extensive discussion relative to this point the reader is referred to Chapter VI in Dobson and Dobson. Humaneness in the Schools: A Neglected Force. Dubuque, Iowa, Kendall/Hunt Publishers, 1976.

TABLE I

THE LANGUAGE OF SCHOOLING

BASIC ELEMENTS	DESIGN A	DESIGN B	DESIGN C
	Movement Toward External Control		Movement Toward Internal Control
		PHILOSOPHY	
Nature of Humankind	Humankind is potentially evil.	Humankind is potentially both good and bad or is a blank slate.	Humankind is potentially good.
Nature of Learning	Truth exists separately from the individual. There are basic facts necessary for all. Learning occurs by reaction.	Truth is relative and subject to the condition of the learner and the environment. Learning occurs by action.	Truth is an individual matter. Learning occurs when the information encountered takes on personal meaning for the learner. Learning occurs by transaction and interaction.
Nature of Knowledge	Logical structure. Information. Subject matter. Vertical relationship. Universal.	Psychological structure. Vertical and horizontal relationships and interrelationships.	Perceptual structure. Relationships and interrelationships. Personal. Gestalt.

37

TABLE I (Continued)

THE LANGUAGE OF SCHOOLING

BASIC ELEMENTS	DESIGN A Movement Toward External Control	DESIGN B	DESIGN C Movement Toward Internal Control
Nature of Society	Closed. Ordered. Institutionalized. Static. Controlling.	In flux. Democratic. Relative values. Experimentation.	Open. Self-reviewing. Individual. Liberating. Distribution. Egalitarian.
Purpose of Education	To understand and apply knowledge. To control the environment. To learn absolute truth.	To Learn prerequisite skills for survival. To learn conditional truths.	To live a full life. To experience the environment. To continue learning personal truth.
		PSYCHOLOGY	
Human Growth and Development	Growth is environmentally determined.	Growth is the realization of one's potential.	Growth is the experiencing of one's potential.

38

Concept of Self	Determined by what others think. Focuses on personality deficiencies.	Determined by how the individual perceives the social environment.	Determined and created by each individual (being--now orientation). (becoming--future orientation).
Human Emotions	Controlled. Closed. Unaware. Masked.	Circumstantial. Objective. Based on position. Well-adjusted.	Free. Open. Spontaneous. Aware. Transparency. Experienced.
Interpersonal Interactions	Role playing. Manipulative games. Defensive. Detached. Distrusting. Dependent.	Minimum risk. Selective. Encountering. Independent.	Sharing. Risking. Trusting. Objective. Exclusive.

OPERATIONS

Curriculum	Predetermined. Structured series. Logical sequence. Content centered. Outcomes established.	Sequenced experiences. Problem-centered. Future utility. Universalism.	Hidden. Unfolding. Created. Process-centered. Unlimited. Emerging. Dynamic.
Instructional Behavior	Transmission of facts and content. Purposeful. Management. Teacher-directed.	Grouping for instructional convenience. Inquiring. Discovering. Open questions with multiple answers. Teacher invitation.	Learner directed. Learner invitation. Teacher functions as source of safety and support.

TABLE I (Continued)

LANGUAGE OF SCHOOLING

BASIC ELEMENTS	DESIGN A	DESIGN B	DESIGN C
	Movement Toward External Control		Movement Toward Internal Control
		OPERATIONS	
Organization	Established. Emphasis on manangement. Focus on homogenous grouping.	Orchestration. Focus on skill grouping.	Changing. Circumstantial. Adaptive. Focus on heterogenous grouping.
Evaluation Techniques	Measurement of facts and content. Determind by authority. Imposed. Product-oriented.	Critical thinking. Problem solving. Tests higher cognitive skills. Focuses on what is learned.	Feedback by invitation. Cooperative pupil and teacher evaluation. Non-damaging comparison. Focuses on how one feels about what is learned as well as on what is learned.

40

	DEFINITION		
Definitions of Curriclum	A structured series of intended learning outcomes. - M. Johnson (1967)	A sequence of potential experiences set up in school for the purpose of disciplining children and youth in group ways of thinking and acting. - Smith, Stanley, Shores (1957)	An attempted definition of humankind translated into educational specifications. - R. Dobson (1976)
Representative Language	Structure. Management. Reinforcement. Shaping. Labeling. Performance. Accountability. Objectives. Behavior. Matching. Environment. Cause-effect. Measurement. Observation. Transmission of Facts. Roles. Function. Control. Intelligence. Reality. Order. Standards. Tests. Grades. Direct.	Sequence. Stages. Growth and Development. Becoming. Correlated. Interest. Programs. Diagnostic. Readiness. Techniques. Skills. Activity. Individual differences. Rational. Well-adjusted. Motivation. Progress. Expectations. Understanding. Discipline. Knowledge. Evaluation. Enable. Support. Facilitate. Guide. Help. Interests. Meaningful.	Being. Desires. Process. Democratic. Freedom. Feedback Fulfillment. Experience. Diversity. Perception. Potential. Harmony. Personal order. Self-direction. Accepting. Unique. Consequences. Awareness. Sharing. Trusting. Allow. Experiment. Involve. Issues. Options. Natural. Spontaneous. Personal meaning.

According to Macdonald (1968, p. 39) "...training is the process of preparing a person to perform defined functions in predictable situations and education is the process of equipping an individual to perform undefined functions in unpredictable situations." An educational program committed to the training end of the continuum is based on the belief that humans are the sum total of their experiences, passive victims of their environments. Conversely, the opposite end of the continuum is committed to the idea that humans are active, goal-seeking organisms eager to profit from encounters with the environment.

The basic elements of the Schooling Dialogue Model (Table I), as they apply to each of the three schools of thought, are categorized into four parts: (a) philosophy, (b) psychology, (c) operations, and (d) definitions. A discussion of the model follows in the remainder of this chapter.

Philosophy

The Nature of Humankind. The philosophy of humankind possessed by people influences how they interact with others. Those who adhere to a Design A profile believe that humankind's potential tends toward evil. Therefore, children must be directed and controlled. These people attempt to shape learners according to their values and teach children what they **should** know.

Inherent in Design B, a neutral belief about humankind, are expressions of restrained warmth as youngsters are maneuvered toward predetermined goals. Design B proponents begin with children where they currently are functioning and manipulate the environment so children have the best possible experiences based upon the adults' perception of what is best. These adults encourage the potential effectiveness of humanity by opening choice making, problem solving, creativity, and autonomy.

People oriented toward Design C believe that humankind's potential is basically good; humans are cooperative and constantly seeking experiences which enhance their unique selves. These people, therefore, accept each child and provide stability as they interact with all others in the school setting.

Nature of Learning. Educators adopting the philosophy of Design A adhere to mental faculty psychology and see the mind as a giant psychological storehouse capable of receiving and holding in cold storage a multitude of facts, concepts, and skills. When the occasion calls for one or another of these particles of learning, the mind delivers it to the stage of action. The development of various skills through drill, practice, habit formation, and conditioning are appropriate methods.

Theories of teaching-learning derived from Design B focus on a blend of the teacher as a manipulator and the intellectual structures characterizing what is to be taught. This approach concentrates on how children think and how their thinking changes with age.

Design C presents experiencing, being, and learning as a totality dichotomized only after the fact. Macdonald, Wolfson, and Zaret (1973, p. 8) established: "Learning emerges in the flow and continuity of man's experiencing and growing; growth is not a statistic process, nor can there be static outcomes of learning."

Nature of Knowledge. It is not uncommon for some curriculum theorists to think of school curriculum as composed of highly separate subjects which have very little relationship to each other. There does not seem to be a clear distinction between what is information and what is ksowledge. Information becomes knowledge only when it takes on personal meaning for the individual.

The nature of knowledge encompasses many questions. How does knowing take place? How do we know what we know? How do we decide what knowledge is worth having? How do we know reality? Answers to these questions are arrived at differently for those subscribing to either Design A, Design B, or Design C.

Those who are proponents of Design A submit the existence of a central body of knowledge which must be transmitted to all. The truth is pre-existent to the learning of it. The most valid way of discovering truth is the empirical method (sense experience). The test of truth is its correspondence to reality.

Design B advocates assert that knowledge is rooted in experience. Individuals "create" knowledge as they interact with the total environment. Knowledge is therefore tentative. As individuals grow, develop, and change, knowledge of what is true will also change. Information becomes knowledge when it is considered relevant to the solution of a particular problem.

Individuals who support Design C submit that the only thing people can be certain of is experiencing a stream of thoughts and feelings. They are in concert with Design B proponents when they propose that truth cannot be established once and for all because individuals are constantly making choices and changing.

Nature of Society. When a society begins to fear that its culture is not important to the young, then it concludes that education must be made to happen. The degree to which the school should seek to reflect or reconstruct the society becomes an issue of great debate.

According to Design A policy, school is one of the most important institutions in society whose purpose is preservation of the culture. In other words, school is the tool for maintaining existing social orders after the public has decided upon them. School does not, however, create social order. The task becomes one of developing a standardized student-citizen as a product of the system.

Conversely, in Design B, society is a process in which individuals participate. The major role of the school is to teach the adults of the future to deal with the planning necessarily involved in the process called society. Education must serve as a source of new ideas.

Design C educators believe the way to improve society is through improving the quality of individuals, not through improving institutions. The school's primary task is individual; that is, the school should concentrate upon the development of freedom in the child. The tendency is toward an egalitarian society.

Purpose of Education. It would seem that the time has come for people from the three basic camps to declare what they see as the purpose of education. Clark and Beatty (1967) ask:

> Do we shape learners according to our values and teach them what they should know? Or, do we foster the potential effectiveness of humanity by open choice making, problem solving, creativity, and autonomy and follow the results wherever they may go? (p. 70)

This is a question seldom asked in educational circles, let alone discussed with any personal intention. The manner in which people respond to this question probably places them in one of the three camps.

If people view their responsibility as one of transmitting to the young universal truth, then they definitely are supporting Design A. If they view truth as relative and subject to time, circumstance, and place and the task of the school as teaching survival skills to the young, then they probably can be classified as Design B proponents. If educators view truth as a personal matter to be established by individuals as they experience their potentials, then they are advocates of Design C.

Psychology

Human Growth and Development. The definition of human growth and development is crucial to formulating a dialogue relative to schooling. Human growth and development, as defined by those with Design A profiles, results in a disease or pathological model. Educators' behaviors resemble those of the medical profession as they focus on deficiencies of youngsters by diagnosing, prescribing, and treating.

If Design A subscribes to a medical model, then Design B subscribes to an agronomy model. Children are viewed as passing through various developmental stages as they move toward maturity. Just as stalks of corn grow toward maturity given adequate soil, sun, and moisture, so it is

44

with young children as they move toward their potentials. The value of current experiences is assessed by their future value.

Design C advocates define human growth and development as the experiencing of one's potential. The present is stressed for its own value. Children are not seen as miniature or pre-adults. Potential is not something one prepares for but rather is something one already is.

Concept of Self. Since growth and development are environmentally determined, then self-concept is ascertained by what others think. This is the Design A stance.

Since proponents of Design B view potential as something to be realized, they purport that self-concept is determined by how the individual receives and interprets information from the environment. Since the emphasis is on becoming, Design B proponents have a future orientation.

In contrast, Design C advocates believe that a concept of self is an extension and expression of self as each experiences his/her potential. The emphasis is on "being" and therefore, Design C proponents have a "now" orientation.

Human Emotions and Interpersonal Interactions. Design A, depicting people as victims of their environments, presents relationships "...as having two alternatives: to control or be controlled" (Shostrom, 1968, p. 24). Therefore, people play roles, maneuver, and conceal motives in interactions with others. People of this belief tend to be passive and quite dependent.

"Well-adjusted" may be a term best describing the Design B profile. Advocates are intent upon programming children toward conformity and adjustment to society and its institutions. Minimum risk and selectivity in interpersonal interactions are descriptive of Design B proponents.

Emotions of Design C advocates are spontaneously and freely expressed. They have the freedom and courage to be, to express their potentials. Self-fulfillment rather than adjustment is a key difference. These people honestly express their feelings in authentic relationships and communicate nonpossessiveness in their involvement with others.

Operations

Curriculum. Curriculum, according to Design A, is predetermined and results in subject matter which is highly structured and logical. Curriculum is definitely content centered.

The curriculum, according to Design B, results in the sequencing of learning experiences which are problem-centered. Future utility and universalism guide the selection of content. The sequencing of content is based on identified stages of growth and development.

In Design C, spontaneous interaction has the potential for unfolding and allowing to emerge an unlimited source of curriculum lying dormant within the learner's creative reservoir. The curriculum is dynamic and emerges as a consequence of the students' needs, wants, and desires.

Instructional Behavior. The instructional behavior of teachers following Design A is reflective of their philosophy of humankind and their beliefs relative to the purpose of education. As a consequence of these beliefs, they attempt to indoctrinate: The transmission of verifiable facts is paramount. Instructional activities are preplanned with specific performance objectives clearly stated.

Teachers advocating Design B use questioning as an instructional strategy, but the questions are open and multiple answers are sought for discussion purposes. Grouping is seen as the way to individualize instruction.

The instructional behavior of the teacher who adheres to Design C is determined by the learner and occurs only by invitation from the learner. In no way does the teacher impose or trespass into the learner's personal space until an invitation has been extended.

Organization. Organizational arrangement according to Design A is rigid and orderly in nature. The emphasis is on management and efficiency. As a consequence of the organizational design being established, time-space becomes segmented; subject-matter is segregated and parceled according to time allotments.

The organization of the school by Design B is an orchestrated expression of the curriculum and instructional arrangement. Subject matter assumes universalism and focuses on utility. Flexible scheduling is related to instructional needs of the staff. Individualized instruction occurs by pacing the students through study sequences.

In Design C, organization is adaptive to the circumstances occurring as a consequence of a time-space blend. Students individually plan their own use of time within limits of personal and social order.

Evaluation. Evaluation in Design A is based on comparisons and is product oriented. The measurement of facts and content is imperative in the evaluation of student learning. Evaluation standards and procedures are determined by an authority and these, in turn, are imposed upon students.

Design B proponents attempt to evaluate critical thinking, problem solving, and higher order cognitive skills. This approach focuses on what is learned and utilizes this information in prescribing future learning tasks.

Evaluation, by Design C, is solicited from the learner and is self-established. Feedback is available upon request and is a shared experience, as opposed to being imposed from without.

Definition

Differing assumptions concerning school functions, what should be taught and how learning should occur, results in at least three varying yet basic definitions of curriculum. These definitions of curriculum were presented in the model. Each of the definitions reflects a different perspective relative to the purpose of school. The definition selected affects the complexion of the educative process provided to, for, or with youngsters.

Summary

Despite limitations, the model presented in this chapter enables those interested in schooling to make useful distinctions among education directions proposed by three basic groups. It is probably safe to say that these directions are seldom, if ever, found in pure form; however, most schools are patterned after one of the three. We hope readers will find the categorizations of the model useful for organizing their thoughts concerning the goals, content, and organization of any school.

References

Clark, R., & Beatty, W. H. (1967). Learning and evaluation. In F. T. Wilhelm (Ed.), Evaluation as feedback and guide (pp. 49-71). Washington, DC: Association of Supervision and Curriculum Development.

Dobson, R. L., & Dobson, J. E. (1976). Humaneness in schools: A neglected force. Dubuque, IA: Kendall/Hunt.

Ebel, R. L. (1972). What are schools for? Phi Delta Kappan, 14, 3-7.

Frazier, A. (1970). Here and now: Points of decision in the quest for a new curriculum. In R. Leeper (Ed.), A man for tomorrow's world (pp. 28-46). Washington, DC: Association for Supervision and Curriculum Development.

Gasset, J. O. Y. (1967). The origin of philosophy. (T. Talbot, Trans.). New York: W. W. Norton.

Johnson, M. (1967). Definitions and models in curriculum theory. Educational Theory, 17(9), 127-131.

Macdonald, J. (1968). A curriculum rationale. In E. Short & G. Marconnit (Eds.), Contemporary thoughts on public school curriculum (pp. 37-41). Dubuque, IA: Wm. C. Brown.

Macdonald, J., Wolfson, B., & Zaret, E. (1973). Reschooling society: A conceptual model. Washington, DC: Association for Supervision and Curriculum Development.

Macdonald, J. (1977, March). Looking toward the future in curriculum. Paper presented at the meeting of the Professors of Curriculum, Houston, TX.

Shostrom, E. (1968). Man, the manipulator. New York: Bantam.

Smith, B., Stanley, W., & Shores, J. (1957). Fundamentals of curriculum. New York: Harcourt, Brace & World.

SECTION III

STATE OF THE ART: RESEARCH ON TEACHING

It has been our contention throughout this book that although educators are concerned about the quality of education in American schools, solutions to problems plaguing the schools have tended toward providing simplistic, technical solutions to complex problems. The part/whole relationship is seen primarily for the isolated parts. This becomes more evident when examining the research literature on teaching-effectiveness/teacher-competency. The next two chapters examine this research.

We believe it is critical for educators to begin questioning the language used in describing schools and what happens there. When researchers begin examining the underlying assumptions of their research questions, broad categories of language metaphors, particularly regarding teaching-effectiveness/teacher-competency research, will be found that seem to dominate the current literature. In examining these metaphors and research categories, educators can better understand the direction of their research efforts and provide a rationale for alternative conceptualizations of schooling.

While acknowledging that teacher-effectiveness/teacher-competency research certainly has its place as a legitimate research endeavor, we suggest the need to expand the paradigm. Educators must look toward the uniqueness of the teacher in order to formulate questions which are less within a technical model of teaching, and more in line with a humanistic, person-centered paradigm.

SECTION II

STATE OF THE ART: RESEARCH ON TEACHING

It seems reasonable to expect teachers to be both competent and effective. Designing the means, however, of determining teaching effectiveness and teacher competence becomes complex. In Chapter 4 we argue that (a) the language of teaching effectiveness and teacher competency research is subtly promoting a technical and political ideology, (b) the efforts of these research activities serve to perpetuate a set of "myths" relative to the teaching experience, and (c) we suggest an alternative focus for teaching effectiveness research—the unique person who teaches. This chapter strengthens the foundation built in previous chapters relative to the power of language in controlling the direction of education and investigates its impact specifically upon teaching-effectiveness research.

CHAPTER 4

THE LANGUAGE OF TEACHING EFFECTIVENESS AND TEACHER COMPETENCY RESEARCH*

Wanting teachers to be effective and competent seems to be a reasonable expectation. However, designing the means of determining teaching effectiveness and teacher competency becomes complex. Traditionally, the major thrust in teaching effectiveness and teacher competency studies has been an emphasis on designing research studies that focus on the technical and political aspects of the teaching-learning experience. Basically, this research includes studies concerned with various instructional methodologies and pupil achievement (Good, Biddle, & Brophy, 1975; Fisher, Mariave, & Filby, 1979; Russell & Fea, 1963), teacher characteristics and teaching effectiveness (Coker, Medley, & Soar, 1980; Getzels & Jackson, 1963; Raskow, Airasian, & Madaus, 1978), and teacher behaviors as related to pupil achievement (Good, 1979; Rosenshine, 1976; Withall & Lewis, 1963).

In these paradigms for studying teaching effectiveness and teacher competency, little attention is focused on the nature of the research questions or why they are posed. To be satisfied with asking the right research question is not enough. Responsible educators must ask why the question was asked and why it was phrased in a particular manner. The scope and nature of research questions cannot be neglected. **Scientific investigation is not value-neutral.** In this chapter we argue that (a) the language of teaching effectiveness and competency research is subtly promoting a technical and political ideology, (b) the effects of these research activities serve to perpetuate a set of "myths" relative to the teaching experience, and finally, (c) we suggest an alternative focus for teaching effectiveness research--the unique person who teaches.

A possible, and often overlooked, explanation causing the study of teaching effectiveness to follow technical lines of investigation may be the language of teaching. The power of language to influence or direct the study of teaching is supported by Soltis (1973), who suggests that a complex educational system develops a specialized vocabulary. As we argued in Chapter 1, educational words have power--the power to direct the procedures and purposes of researchers. Typical words used in research on teaching effectiveness are behavior (student and teacher), effectiveness, personality, achievement, outcomes, interaction, characteristics, behavioral measurements, and performance. More recently, the literature is using such words as direct instruction, time on task, assignments, expectation, monitoring, pupil task involvement, seat

---

*This chapter is an edited version of our article which first appeared in Viewpoints in Teaching and Learning, 58(2) (Spring, 1982), 23-33. Copyright 1982 VTL.

work, and a whole host of terms reflecting technical and political value bases. As was demonstrated in Chapter I, the metaphorical bases of these words are industrial, military, and disease (medical). For example:

Industrial - classroom management, cost effectiveness, efficiency, institutional planning, programming, output measures, product, feedback, defective, input-process-output, quality control, time management.

Military - target population, information system, centralization of power, line and staff, scheduling, discipline, objectives, teaching strategies, maintain.

Disease - diagnosis, treatment, prescription, remediation, monitor, label, deviant, impaired, referral-procedure, special needs.

These metaphors encourage teaching-learning research to be viewed and investigated from a technical perspective. Researchers invented words to serve as tools and now they are controlled by these tools. In Chapter I we pointed out that language which is intended to explain or describe reality too often becomes the reality. What cannot be explained with language is often ignored and ultimately dismissed. **Words serve to produce a paradoxical situation, namely, the freezing and unfreezing of reality.** Unfortunately, within the field of education, the words used tend to provide a freezing function. We submit that this is due to the technical emphasis on defining terms, along with the emphasis on observable behavior to explain the human condition. Building on what was written in Chapter 3, we propose that if researchers are to pursue the roots of reality relative to teaching-learning, they must uncover the meaning of words blurred by custom and usage. Researchers of teaching effectiveness are affected by language and, more often than not, their research efforts reflect the posed meaning these words possess.

As expressed by Frymier (1972, p. 13), there are languages of conditional relationships and relationships "without conditions": the first is a language of "control"; the second is a language of "love and growth." One has to wonder if teaching effectiveness research has as its priority control or learning (love and growth). Roberts (1976, p. 321) echoed this sentiment when she wrote, "It is impossible to practice the ideas of Skinner and Chomsky simultaneously."

Huebner (1966) discusses the dangers involved in the languaging activity. He refers to the language of the technical model in education as the prevailing focus during the past few years. Huebner, according to Macdonald (1977, p. 15), "...opens the possibilities of political, aesthetic, and moral talk."

We contend that the language of the technical model applied to teaching effectiveness research has contributed to a simplistic, input/output understanding of educational experiences ("student-as-product" orientation). The technical model, along with the language of technical rationale suggests that the "right mix" of technique and content will significantly increase student performance. Teaching is viewed as a "science and technology" with identifiable skills lending themselves to short-term teaching goals that focus on a utilitarian perspective. Tabachnick, Popkowitz and Zeichner (1979-80) suggest that this leads to a managerial understanding of teaching.

The language of the technical model applied to teaching effectiveness suggests scientific accuracy and predictability, and the nature of this model has an interest in control (management and engineering). The historical roots of this orientation have been outlined by others (Apple, 1979; Giroux, 1980; Kliebard, 1975). Tabachnick et al. (1979-80, p. 16), in their research on the student-teaching experience, observed student teachers engaged in the "...routine and mechanistic teaching of precise and short-term skills and in management activities designed to keep the class quiet, orderly, and on task."

Giroux (1980) suggests that the political nature of education programs is seen in the language used to address everyday school practices. Stating that teacher education programs serve as socializing agencies embodying "...rules and patterns for constructing and legitimizing categories regarding competence, achievement and success," (p. 8) he suggests that this, in turn, serves to define specific teacher roles

...through the language they use and the assumptions and research they consider essential to the teaching profession. The basic premises and rules that underlie such programs are usually viewed as commonsense perceptions; they go unquestioned and often result in many problems in the teaching arena to be defined as basically technical ones. (p. 8)

In the same vein, Foshay (1980) proclaims the importance of language and its linkage to practice. He states:

It is scarcely recognized the way we talk and think has a controlling effect. Behind our manifest language is a metaphor, which carries latent meanings to events. Behind our action is also theory about the domain of action. (p. 82)

Foshay's contention provides a clear picture of how theory and practice, talk and action are underlying sequences in everyday events and, quite possibly, research efforts. Haplin (1969) lends support when he states:

But if the word is only as good as the idea behind it, we as educators should ask ourselves more frequently than we do, not just what does this or that educational word mean, but to what assumptions, values, theories, procedures, and strategies for teaching do these words commit us. (p. 335)

We submit that either certain words used in teaching-learning research have generated myths about teaching effectiveness, or certain myths about teaching have generated certain word usage. Causal priority does not seem particularly important. What is important is that currently used "buzz words" connote a simplistic technical view of teaching-learning.

Unfounded Teaching Myths

The study of the practice of teaching is to a large degree grounded in conventional wisdom--a perspective with questionable validity. This conventional wisdom is based on a set of assumptions, some of which have not been validated. Logical and scientific expressions of faulty assumptions do nothing more than intensify the possibility of error. The result is a vast amount of research serving to perpetuate a set of myths relative to the practice of teaching. Combs (1979, p. 2) states that, "A myth is a widely held belief that is not true." However, a myth can be partially true. Therein lies the danger.

The following are examples of myths or unfounded truisms relative to teaching effectiveness and teacher competency that remain illusive because for some reason many researchers have avoided questioning what "everybody" seems to know:

I.   **The "universal" teacher.** The existence of a single model of teaching effectiveness or teacher competency is a prevailing misconception. Such a model is predicated upon the assumption that it is possible to predict all of the human interactions which will occur in teaching-learning situations. There are no pat answers to if-then teacher-student encounters; at best there are only viable alternatives. Few, if any, teacher educators espouse the "universal" teacher concept--yet, for some reason, there seems to be an almost pathological preoccupation with perfecting such a model.

2.   **The xerox model of teacher education.** West (1972) states that schools have sanctioned an organizational farce by assuming that all teachers are alike in needs, abilities, and aspirations: A teacher is not "...a carbon copy of his colleagues" (p. 249). He continues by stating that

56

because schools tend to view teachers as if they were cast from the same mold, many teachers experience loss of identity and alienation from self. The result is that schools benefit neither the students nor the teachers. Only when teachers are aware of and sensitive to themselves and reciprocal influences is it possible to alter the teaching-learning situation. Therefore, we submit, any radical change in teacher education will necessarily take into consideration the introduction of the unique person of the teacher into the classroom.

3. **The role access model.** The concept of role behavior is based on a narrow view of the nature of persons. The notion, by necessity, is derived from a static concept of personality. Many current attempts at improving teaching performance (staff development) can be labeled "role access" efforts. Improvement is seen as an increase in the number of role behaviors to which teachers have access and which they can perform successfully. When change does occur with this approach, one set of role behaviors is simply exchanged for another set. The person in the process may or may not have changed (Dobson, Dobson, & Kessinger, 1980).

4. **Viewing change as an event.** Change can be described from at least two perspectives: (a) as an event with identifiable and observable behavioral modifications, or (b) as a process which suggests movement toward increased awareness of self-potential in life-profiting situations. Change as an event is short-range in longevity, ususally diminishing upon removal of stimuli causing the modification. Change as a process is subject to internalization, thus becoming integrated as a part of total self. Schmeck (1981, p. 384) suggests that deep processing involves "devoting more attention to the meaning and classification of an idea suggested by a symbol than to the symbol itself."

Change as a process takes time, is a highly personal experience, and is developmental in nature (Shallcross, 1980). Institutions cannot change until individual people within them change. Thus, the uniqueness of the individual person must by necessity be the primary target of interventions designed to improve teaching performance. In reporting on the RAND Change Agent study, McLaughlin and March (1978-79, p. 65) state, "We have learned that the problem of reform or change is more of a function of people and organizations than of technology."

5. **Teaching as a product.** This approach can be demonstrated by the use of a single evaluation instrument to judge all teachers' performances according to predetermined criteria. The futility of a single performance scale is overwhelming when one considers that Joyce (1978) has identified 80 different teaching models.

To recapitulate, while we admit there are certain teaching skills which can be taught and measured, we reject the idea that teaching is fundamentally comprised of the right mix of techniques, methods, and skills. As a result of the profession becoming an increasingly highly skilled technology with a primary emphasis on method (Peters, 1977), researchers have by and large restricted their focus to areas amenable to this technology, thus creating a vocabulary insensitive to the human dimension of the teaching-learning experience. **Narrowness of perspective for the sake of research efficiency does little to contribute to a needed body of knowledge.**

Alternative Paradigm

There is a vast difference between developing and implementing a personal philosophy, a psychological posture, an emotional state, and concentrating on how to perfect one's role performance. Humans are the inventors of ideas and definitions of self and these ideas and self-definitions are the beacons guiding daily lives and ultimately affecting the degree to which persons experience self as well as others. To succumb to an imposed reality is to experience the loss or prostitution of personal validation, resulting in alienation from self as well as others, thus leading to role behaviors which may be inauthentic (Dobson & Dobson, & Kessinger, 1980).

Therefore, any paradigm of teaching effectiveness must take into account belief-practice congruency with regard to philosophic beliefs, emotional awareness, and psychological posture. This requires an emphasis upon the uniqueness of individual people. Teachers are first of all people, far more than descriptions of their role behaviors. The remainder of this chapter discusses what we believe should be the focus of teaching effectiveness and teacher competency research--the unique person who teaches.

The teacher's personal philosophy. Individuals possess philosophies of life whether or not they are cognizant of them. Teachers' philosophies, personal values, and beliefs form the foundations from which they make choices or decisions relative to their personal and professional lives. Hunter (1979) emphasizes that teaching is decision making and Peterson (1979) reports that the process of teacher decision making is an increasingly potent area for research.

Basic to a teacher's personal philosophy is his/her belief in human nature or a belief about people and how they develop. Helping professions research (Combs, 1969) concludes the system of beliefs that helpers hold of others is an extremely important variable in their effectiveness and beliefs enable helpers to be spontaneous in their transactions with others. Purkey and Avila (1971) also emphasize that teachers' beliefs concerning the worth and dignity of individuals are paramount and that in order to identify good and poor teaching it is necessary to explore how teachers see themselves and the world around them.

Usher and Hanke (1971, p. 3) recommend educators attempt to understand effective teachers from a "self as instrument" approach. Teaching effectiveness is a personal matter involving the effective use of one's unique self. They emphasize that the nature and quality of teachers'

58

personal beliefs become crucial, for teachers convey their bel'
their methods, knowledge, and procedures or in spite
procedures used in the classroom. Goodlad (1977) echoes this sentimen
and calls upon teachers to examine beliefs and to act responsibly so they
do not violate their own integrity. According to Katz and Stotland (1959),
values are a highly integrated set of attitudes about particular objects in
an individual's environment. One's values are generally lasting and deep-
seated beliefs. Today, educators realize that value neutrality on the part
of the teacher is an impossibility (Apple, 1979; Freire, 1970). If teachers
cannot maintain neutrality, then they must be aware of the values they
espouse or portray.

Values are an important element in an individual's life. And yet,
many schools do not provide the freedom nor encourage teachers to
express and live by their own values. Teachers are often forced to accept
or at least to play roles in which they accept the values of a particular
school system in order to keep their jobs. Therefore, teachers may be
engaging in self-betrayal of values (Moustakas, 1967) and forcing
themselves to fit into another's plans, to interact with others in ways that
have no personal meaning.

Inherent to a teacher's personal philosophy are assumptions about
the purpose of schooling, the nature of knowledge, society, and the
person's position within that society. These views have an effect on what
a teacher does in the classroom. How teachers organize curriculum,
evaluate and interact with students, and view themselves within the
teaching-learning context is affected by the basic philosophical
orientation they bring to the classroom.

The relationship between teachers' philosophies of human nature
(beliefs and values) and selected educational variables is an area of
research worthy of expanded analysis. Additional research is needed to
identify these variables and their interrelations.

The teacher's emotional awareness. The personal sensitivity of
teachers, the awareness of attitudes and feelings they experience from
moment to moment, as well as their awareness of the attitudes and
feelings students are experiencing, are tremendous influences in the
classroom. What the teacher is experiencing at the moment of
interaction with a student will influence his/her tone of voice, rate of
speech, facial expressions and gestures, as well as verbal content. What
the student is experiencing at the time of the interaction will definitely
influence his/her acceptance of the teacher's message and the response.
Therefore, attention must be paid to the sensitivity of the teacher, not
only because it influences the communication processes within the
classroom but because sensitivity or lack of sensitivity to self and others
influences one's personal growth.

We contend that the feelings experienced in a classroom, whether they are positive (happiness, excitement, acceptance) or negative (anger, frustration, rejection), influence not only personal and social growth but also the academic growth of students. Leonard (1968) suggests that certain social conditions encourage the ignoring of emotions and the distrusting of one's own feelings. Dahms (1972) reinforces this view by suggesting that people are taught to suppress and control feelings rather than to express them. He presents an argument for emotional intimacy as a basic requirement for true human survival.

Hamachek (1969) relates that good teachers view teaching as primarily a human process involving human relationships and human meanings. He continues that flexibility and the ability to perceive the world from the student's point of view seem to distinguish more effective from less effective teachers. Therefore, we propose that teaching effectiveness research focus on teacher sensitivity or emotional awareness.

The teacher's psychological posture. How teachers feel about themselves, their psychological postures, definitely influences what does or does not happen in the classroom. The fears or insecurities some teachers possess concerning their own personal worth may create barriers to honest personal encounters with youngsters (Dobson & Dobson, 1976).

Most educators will argue that self-concept, the image a person holds of self, is not objective and does influence thoughts, perceptions, and behaviors. The developmental aspect of self-concept has been described by many researchers (Allport, 1937; Engle, 1959; Purkey, 1970). The self-concept serves as a guide or a reference point for one's behavior (Glock, 1972). Therefore, all that a person experiences is filtered through and mediated by the self-concept, an image one has learned from significant others over the years. Since one's perceptions of self are learned over a period of time, they are quite resistant to change (Purkey, 1978).

As a result of past experiences, teachers develop certain expectancies about their behaviors. In a review of the literature relative to the effects of expectancies of self and others on actual behavior, Brickman (1966) derived two generalizations: (a) People who expect to fail are most likely to fail even when they succeed and desire success; and (b) If people do perform well, they are more likely to discount the evidence of their success. Brickman believes this occurs because behaviors that disconfirm expectations lead an individual to feel dissatisfied and uncomfortable. As a result, individuals desire to live up to their own expectations.

If the self-concept serves as a guide and mediator of perceptions, thoughts, and actions, then the image a teacher has of self is of utmost importance. Hamachek (1969), and Dieken and Fox (1973) suggest that if it is true that good teachers have postive views of themselves and others, then more opportunities should be provided for both preservice and inservice teachers to acquire positive self-perceptions. A potent area for research is the extent to which the school climate affects positive self-perceptions.

Conclusion

In the final analysis, words have the power to explain. They also have the power to dictate thought, or ultimately to freeze reality. Has the study of teaching effectiveness and teacher competency been frozen in scientific, technical, and political value communities and neglected the aesthetic and ethical (Huebner, 1966)?

The primary question is not one of teaching effectiveness or ineffectiveness. The question is one of representative language from value communities and concomitant constructs utilized in arriving at judgments about teaching effectiveness and teacher competency. What is needed is revitalized language resulting in the creation of new, or the revitalization of old, constructs or paradigms for studying teaching effectiveness and teacher competency. This can be realized by shifting from an overemphasis on scientific, technical, and political language to aesthetic and ethical language. This, in turn, can facilitate the creation of new language or the remixing of old language to arrive at new constructs. In other words, in reference to teaching effectiveness and teacher competency, we do not need new thought. What we need are new ways of thinking about what we have already thought.

Schools are complex social organizations; thus, simplistic approaches to improving the quality of school life are ineffective. A review of the literature suggests that the unique person of the teacher is a most important factor in the learning process and that a teacher's philosophy, emotional awareness, and psychological posture form the foundation from which he/she makes choices and decisions about the teaching-learning experience. Therefore, any radical change in teaching effectiveness will necessarily involve introducing the unique person of the teacher into the classroom.

In the next chapter we examine more closely the different approaches to studying teaching effectiveness and argue that research dominating the field today tends to encourage professional immaturity.

61

References

Allport, G. W. (1937). Personality: A psychological interpretation. New York: Holt, Rinehart & Winston.

Apple, M. (1979). Ideology and curriculum. London: Routledge & Kegan Paul, Ltd.

Brickman, P. (1966, December). Performance expectations and performance. Unpublished manuscript, University of Michigan, Research Center for Group Dynamics, Ann Arbor.

Coker, H., Medley, D. M., & Soar, R. S. (1980). How valid are expert opinions about effective teaching? Phi Delta Kappan, 62, 131-134.

Combs, A. W. (Ed.). (1969). Florida studies in the helping professions. Social Science Monograph, (Report No. 37). Gainesville: University of Florida Press.

Combs, A. W. (1979). Myths in education. Boston: Allyn & Bacon.

Dahms, A. M. (1972). Emotional intimacy. Boulder, CO: Pruett.

Dieken, E. H., & Fox, R. B. (1973). Self-perceptions of teachers and their verbal behavior in the classroom. Educational Leadership, 30, 445-449.

Dobson, J. E., & Dobson, R. L. (1980). School climate and the person of the teacher. The Networker, 3, 23-27.

Dobson, R. L., & Dobson, J. E. (1976). Humaneness in schools: A neglected force. Dubuque, IA: Kendall/Hunt.

Dobson, R. L., Dobson, J. E., & Kessinger, J. O. (1980). Staff development: A humanistic approach. Lanham, MD: University Press of America.

Engle, M. (1959). The stability of the self-concept in adolescence. Journal of Abnormal Social Psychology, 58, 211-216.

Fisher, C., Mariave, R., & Filby, N. (1979). Improving teaching by increasing academic learning time. Educational Leadership, 37, 52-54.

Foshay, A. W. (1980). Curriculum Talk. In A. Foshay (Ed.), Considered action for curriculum improvement (pp. 82-94). Washington, DC: Association for Supervision and Curriculum Development.

Freire, P. (1970). Pedagogy of the oppressed. New York: Seabury Press.

Frymier, J. R. (1972). A curriculum manifesto. Oceanside, OR: Curriculum Bulletin.

Getzels, J. H., & Jackson, P. W. (1963). The teacher's personality and characteristics. In N. L. Gage (Ed.), Handbook of research on teaching (pp. 506-582). Chicago: University of Chicago Press.

Giroux, H. A. (1980). Teacher education and the ideology of social control. Journal of Education, 162(1), 5-27.

Glock, M. (1972). Is there a pygmalion in the classroom? The Reading Teacher, 25(5), 405-409.

Good, T. (1979). Teacher effectiveness in the elementary school: What we know about it now. Journal of Teacher Education, 30, 52-64.

Good, T., Biddle, B., & Brophy, J. (1975). Teachers make a difference. New York: Holt, Rinehart & Winston.

Goodlad J. (1977, April). The trouble with humanistic education. Paper presented at the Fourth National Conference on Humanistic Education, Carrollton, GA.

Hamachek, D. (1969). Characteristics of good teachers and implications for teacher education. Phi Delta Kappan, 50, 341-344.

Haplin, A. (1969). Change the mythology. Theory Into Practice, 8, 334-338.

Huebner, D. (1966). Curriculum language and classroom meanings. In J. Macdonald & R. Leeper (Eds.), Language and meaning (pp. 8-26). Washington, DC: Association for Supervision and Curriculum Development.

Hunter, M. (1979). Teaching is decision making. Educational Leadership, 37, 62-67.

Joyce, B. (1978). Selecting learning experiences. Washington, DC: Association for Supervision and Curriculum Development.

Katz, D. E., & Stotland, E. (1959). A preliminary statement to a theory of attitude structure and change. In S. Koch (Ed.), Psychology: A study of science, Vol. 3: Formulations of the person and the social context (pp. 69-92). New York: McGraw-Hill.

Kliebard, H. (1975). Bureaucracy and curriculum theory. In W. Pinar (Ed.), Curriculum theorizing: the reconceptualists (pp. 51-69). Berkeley: McCutchan.

Leonard, G. (1968). Education and ecstasy. New York: Delacorte.

Macdonald, J. (1977). Values bases and issues for curriculum. In A. Molnar & J. Zahorich (Eds.), Curriculum theory (pp. 10-21). Washington, DC: Association of Supervision and Curriculum Development.

McLaughlin, M., & March, D. (1978-79). Staff development and school change. In A. Lieberman & L. Miller (Eds.), Staff development: New demands, new realities, new perspectives (pp. 43-67). New York: Teachers College, Columbia University.

Moustakas, C. (1967). The authentic teacher. Cambridge, MA: Howard A. Doyle.

Peters, R. S. (1977). Must an educator have an aim? In A. Bellack & H. Kliebard (Eds.), Curriculum and evaluation (pp. 123-130). Berkeley: McCutchan.

Peterson, P. (1979). Direct instruction: Effective for what and for whom? Educational Leadership, 37, 46-48.

Purkey, W. W. (1970). Self-concept and school achievement. Englewood Cliffs, NJ: Prentice-Hall.

Purkey, W. W. (1978). Inviting school success. Belmont, CA: Wadsworth.

Purkey, W. W., & Avila, D. (1971). Classroom discipline: A new approach. The Elementary School Journal, 71, 325-328.

Raskow, E., Airasian, P., & Madaus, G. (1978). Assessing school and program effectiveness: Estimating teacher level effects. Journal of Educational Measurement, 15, 15-21.

Roberts, J. (1976). Freedom, the child, the teacher: A gap between ideas and actions. Theory Into Practice, 15, 319-325.

Rosenshine, B. (1976). Recent research on teaching behaviors and student achievement. Journal of Teacher Education, 27, 61-64.

Russell, D. H., & Fea, H. R. (1963). Research on teaching reading. In N. L. Gage (Ed.), Handbook of research on teaching (pp. 865-928). Chicago: University of Chicago Press.

Shallcross, D. J. (1980). Teaching creative behavior. Englewood Cliffs, NJ: Prentice-Hall.

Schmeck, R. R. (1981). Improving learning by improving thinking. Educational Leadership, 38, 384-387.

Soltis, J. F. (1973). The passion to teach. Theory into Practice, 12, 46-49.

Tabachnick, R., Popkowitz, S., & Zeichner, K. M. (1979-80). Teacher education and the professional perspectives of student teachers. Interchange, 10, 12-29.

Usher, R., & Hanke, J. (1971). The "third force" in psychology and college teacher effectiveness research at the University of Northern Colorado. Colorado Journal of Educational Research, 10, 2-9.

West, P. T. (1972). Self-actualization resolving the indivdual-organization conflict. Clearing House, 47, 249-252.

Withall, J., & Lewis, W. W. (1963). Social interaction in the classroom. In N. L. Gage (Ed.), Handbook of research on teaching (pp. 683-714). Chicago: University of Chicago Press.

There are three clearly identifiable and distinctly different approaches to studying teaching effectiveness. One of these approaches is dominating the field, one is receiving token attention, and the third is almost totally ignored. In this chapter we present a brief description and critique of each of these three approaches. Finally, we argue that teaching effectiveness research currently dominating the field serves to encourage professional immaturity.

CHAPTER 5

TEACHING EFFECTIVENESS RESEARCH:
IMPLICATIONS FOR PROFESSIONAL DEVELOPMENT

> Whatever we do in teaching depends
> upon what we think people are like.
> The goals we seek, the things we do,
> the judgments we make, even the
> experiments we are willing to try, are
> determined by our beliefs about the
> nature of man and his capacities. It
> has always been so.
>
> —Arthur Combs

The above statement appeared more than twenty years ago in the Association for Supervision and Curriculum Development Yearbook, Perceiving, Behaving, Becoming (1962). A perusal of current literature on teaching effectiveness research demonstrates that the significance of this statement is being diminished. We view this as unfortunate.

During the past two decades three distinctly different approaches to the study of teaching effectiveness have been established. The research currently dominating the field reflects a technical rationale. Research efforts receiving token attention cluster around what is commonly referred to as humanistic teaching. An almost totally ignored area of research can be appropriately labeled person-centered teaching. The assertion that research related to the study of teaching effectiveness can be classified as either dominant, token, or ignored is dramatized when one examines the Encyclopedia of Educational Research (1982) and finds only one (Combs, 1962) humanistic reference listed under the sections titled Teaching Characteristics (Ryan & Phillips, 1982), and Teaching Effectiveness (Medley, 1982). The references listed for these two sections are studies reflecting a technical model while person-centered teaching effectiveness research is not reported. Additionally, the informed reader will recognize that most major educational journals devoted to reporting teaching effectiveness research have followed a similar posture over the past decade.

This chapter has a dual purpose. First, we present a brief description and critique of the three previously mentioned approaches to studying teaching effectiveness. Secondly, we argue that an exaggerated dependence on a technically based model for investigating the notion of teaching effectiveness serves to perpetuate professional immaturity (Eisner, 1983).

Three Research Approaches

Dominant Research: Technical. As was discussed in the preceding chapter, the majority of research on teaching effectiveness has focused on studies concerned with instructional methodologies and pupil achievement (Anderson, Evertson & Brophy, 1979; Fisher, Mariave, & Filby, 1979; Good, Biddle, & Brophy, 1975; Russell & Fea, 1963), teacher characteristics and teaching effectiveness (Brophy, 1979; Coker, Medley, & Soar, 1980; Getzels & Jackson, 1963; Raskow, Airasian, & Madaus, 1978), and teacher behaviors as related to pupil achievement (Good, 1979; Joyce & Weil, 1980; Rosenshine, 1976; Withall & Lewis 1963).

Studies of teaching of this nature have followed a technical-political model based on a scientific, rational explanation of human behavior. This approach to explaining effective teaching performance suggests that the proper blending of technique and content will significantly increase student performance. This positivistic attitude views teaching as a scientific technology with identifiable, observable skills considered to be the "practice" of teaching. While we are willing to admit there are certain teaching skills which can be taught and measured, we reject the notion that teaching is fundamentally comprised of the proper blend of techniques, methods, and skills.

In Chapter 4 we pointed out that the technical-political model applied to teaching effectiveness suggests precise reasoning ("scientific accuracy") and predictability, and the nature of this model has an interest in control through management procedures. As the teaching profession has become an increasingly highly skilled technology with a primary emphasis on methods and outcomes, teachers have been rewarded for guiding their practice in ways amenable to this technology. As Macdonald suggests (1975), this notion implies that "teachers are potentially interchangeable," and leads to viewing productive activity as something learned and performed "mechanistically." Thus, any "good" teaching activity can be reproduced by any other teacher, and "...all productive teaching is measureable in terms of the criteria of the accountability in use" (pp. 79-80).

Apple (1982) refers to this as a process of "deskilling-reskilling" teachers:

> As the procedures of technical control enter into the school in the guise of pre-designed curricular/teaching/evaluation 'systems,' teachers are being deskilled. Yet they are also being reskilled in a way that is quite consequential. ...while the deskilling involves the loss of craft, the ongoing atrophication of educational skills, the reskilling involves substitution of the skills with ideological visions of management. (p. 256)

Tom (1977) contends that what is lacking in the managerial perspective is the acknowledgment of interpersonal or social relationships:

...these relationships cannot be reduced to a collection of techniques without debasing them and stripping them of their humanity. However, even if one rejects this humanistic concern, there is another fundmental problem. A technology must have definite ends toward which its activity is aimed. There is, of course, no long-term consensus on the aims of education. (p. 78)

The lack of consensus on the aims of education within the technical model is not viewed as problematic because there are commonsense understandings of purpose within the model. The position here becomes one of value-neutrality, that is, teaching and learning as apolitical.

Token Research: Humanistic. Running concurrently with the evolution of a technical-rationale as a base for studying teaching effectiveness have been research efforts reflecting a humanistic model. This movement is receiving little more than token attention (Peters, 1977; West, 1972). Research studies sensitive to the human aspects of the teaching-learning experience have included teacher expectancy studies (Davidson & Lang, 1960; Rosenthal & Jacobson, 1968). The process of perceiving which preceeds expectations is unique to each individual. Bruner (1958) contends that humans tend to maintain a consonance of their opinions, ideas and attitudes. Individuals, therefore, attempt to minimize surprise by imposing a subjective consistency upon their environments.

The psychological credibility of the self-fulfilling phenomenon is perhaps one reason that research has continued despite the failure of Rosenthal and Jacobson to provide totally convincing evidence (Braun, 1973). Neither Snow (1969) nor Thorndike (1968) deny the fact that teacher expectation may be a powerful force. Additional impetus has been provided by studies lending support to that phenomenon (Brophy & Good, 1970; Mendoza, Good, & Brophy, 1971).

Interpersonal relationship studies and writings by Aspy and Roebuck (1980, 1982, 1983), Combs (1969), Dieken and Fox (1973), and Peterson (1979) can also be classified as humanistic literature currently receiving only token attention. After a review of the literature, Hamachek (1969) states that effective teachers appear to be those who are human in the fullest sense. They have a sense of humor, are fair, empathic, more democratic than autocratic, and are able to relate easily and naturally to students on a one-to-one and group basis.

Research relative to learning climate (Anderson & Walberg, 1967; Combs, 1982; Dobson, Grey, & Dobson, 1979; Sinclair, 1968) seems to indicate the need for caring, understanding, openness, acceptance, and genuineness. Rogers (1983) calls attention to the significance of research done from a humanistic perspective when he states:

> ...this research provides convincing evidence--from two teams based on two continents--showing that students learn more, attend school more often, are more creative, more capable of problem solving, when the teachers provide the kind of human, facilitative climate that has been described.... (p. 197)

Aspy and Roebuck (1983, p. 199) further support Roger's statement when they submit that their findings can be summarized with one statement: "...students learn more and behave better when they receive high levels of understanding, caring, and genuiness, than when they are given low levels of them."

Ignored Research: Person-Centered. While these two distinctly different research approaches to the study of teaching effectiveness have been occurring, a third and almost totally ignored area of research also has been conducted. This seemingly ignored research effort can be labeled as person-centered.

Beginning with Dewey (1910, 1964), there has gradually emerged a group of educators who have come to view teachers' philosophies as the basis for their decisions about the educational process. Dewey believed that humans are in a state of change and that goodness resides in them. The signifcance of Dewey's thesis is amplified by Freire (1981) when he states, "Our pedagogy cannot do without a vision of man and the world" (p. 338).

There is ample evidence to suggest that relatively few teachers have developed internally consistent philosophies, that is teaching behaviors that are in accordance with their professed beliefs (Brown, 1968; Kessinger, 1980; Wright, 1980). Marshall (1973) contends that teachers proceed with an eclectic approach comprised of bits of data from diverse psychological and philosophical camps.

Considering this state of the art, it seems that a more systematic treatment of teacher beliefs-practice congruency relative to instruction would be useful. Wiles and Bondi (1979) suggest that educational philosophies are the heart of purposeful activity. They contend that because teachers are confronted with multiple choices for schooling the young, it is vital that teachers understand their own values and beliefs about schooling.

Morris (1966) states:

A limited contingent of educators who have come to see the philosophical and educational problems as continuous has emerged. Philosophy and education are really two aspects of the same undertaking...the forming of those fundamental dispositions toward nature and our fellow man which the world demands of us. This has led to a going beyond educational aims and strategies to examine the relevance of a person's philosophical thinking in curriculum design, teaching methodology, and other areas such as administrative policy-making. (p. 76)

Since teachers play a significant role in determining the educational environment, it is important to know something about their assumptions relative to the nature of humans. Wrightsman (1964) contends that the assumptions one holds about what people are really like influence one's interactions with others. Kelley and Rasey (1952) point out that teachers' basic beliefs about the nature of humans help to define their relationships with students. Combs (1962, 1982) further emphasizes the importance of a person's basic beliefs about the nature of humankind and the influence of this phenomenon upon human interaction in the educational process.

Social scientists have come to realize that people's assumptions about the nature of humankind can be conceptualized and measured, and it can be determined if these beliefs influence behavior toward others. Wrightsman (1964, 1974) developed an instrument for measuring people's beliefs relative to the nature of humankind, the Philosophies of Human Nature Scale (PHN). Research using the PHN has been conducted in the areas of making judgments of specific persons; belief differentiation among occupational groups, sex, family background, religious preferences, authoritarianism, and attitude change; children's perceptions of the educational environment; non-verbal communication patterns; verbal-nonverbal congruency in the classroom; moral development; and pupil control ideology (Childress & Dobson, 1973; Deal, Dobson, & Dobson, 1982; Dobson, Hopkins, & Elsom, 1973; Dobson, Sewell, & Shelton, 1974; Mason, 1967; Wrightsman, 1974). These studies have attempted to identify and measure certain basic beliefs about the nature of humankind and have contributed normative data to the problem of interpersonal aspects of humans. Therefore, the results of this literature emphasize that the basic beliefs one holds about the nature of humankind comprise a viable force in the structuring of reciprocal interactions among people.

As we argued in the preceding chapter, inherent in a teacher's personal philosophy are assumptions about the purposes of schooling, the nature of knowledge, a view of society, and the person's position within that society. These views have an effect on what a teacher does in the classroom. How teachers organize curriculum, evaluate students, interact with students, and view themselves within the teaching-learning context are all affected by the basic philosophical orientation they bring to the classroom. Zeichner's (1979a, 1979b, 1980, 1981) research on the student teaching experience, teacher socialization, and reflective teaching provides a rationale and direction for further research which we believe falls within the person-centered approach.

Research Approaches and Professional Development

The thesis that teachers progress through developmental stages in their careers has been advanced (Castle, 1982; Katz, 1977; Seay, 1982; Shallcross, 1979). Shallcross (1979), using Land's (1973) theory of transformation of the stages of growth of all living things, identified four developmental stages of teaching. The four stages identified by Land and interpreted by Shallcross (1979) are:

1. **Formative** (oneness): an egocentric stage in which the self must learn to feel secure.

2. **Normative** (sameness): replicates teaching behaviors observed in others, desires a sense of belonging, does not want to be thought of as different.

3. **Integrative** (differentness): appreciates differentness in self and others, feels pride in own uniqueness.

4. **Transformational** (change): the existential leap into uncertainty, the beginning of another cycle and new struggles for identity and space.

Figure I is an attempt to compare the three different approaches of teaching effectiveness research identified in this chapter with the Shallcross model of professional development. We argue that research questions, findings, and recommendations identified with the dominant technical-political model of teaching effectiveness are somewhat limited to the early stages of professional development. Humanistic research efforts (token) seem to be associated with stage 2 with some overlapping into stage 3. Finally, teaching effectiveness research which is being virtually ignored (person-centered) can be aligned with stage 4 of the model.

Let us examine the assumption that maximized use of a technical and politically based model for studying teaching effectiveness is apt to encourage professional immaturity. Weller's (1977) educational metaphors—instrumental, tribal, and organic—can be used to assess the accuracy of this assumption which is represented in Figure I. Effective teaching as identified by those who study the technical aspects of that act, is limited to characteristics associated with stages I and 2. Weller (1977) tends to support this assertion when he states:

74

	Stage 1	Stage 2	Stage 3	Stage 4
	Formative (oneness)	**Normative** (sameness)	**Integrative** (differentness)	**Transformational** (change)
	Technical Teaching	Humanistic Teaching	Person-Centered Teaching	
	(Dominant Research)	(Token Research)	(Ignored Research)	
	Instrumental	Tribal	Organic	

Figure 1. A developmental perspective of teaching effectiveness research.

The instrumental metaphor implies an objective to be shaped or changed in particular ways, an instrument (be it tool, machine, or human being) used in appropriate fashion, and certain criteria for determining effective or efficient accomplishment. (p. 12)

Weller's (1977) interpretation of the tribal metaphor can be used to describe characteristics associated with teaching effectiveness research that is seen as humanistic (token). The emphasis at this stage is on the culture (school). He contends:

In the context of humanistic education the objectives may derive from the traditions, values, and understandings of a particular culture, frequently represented by time-honored disciplines that convey knowledge and meaning. This educational metaphor operates within the human interests of consensus - mutual understanding, group identity.... (p. 16)

Person-centered teaching effectiveness research (ignored) is identified with the later time span of stage 3 and then stage 4 of the developmental model and can be represented with an organic metaphor. Again, we borrow from Weller (1977) who states: "One might say that this metaphor operates within the human interest in liberation--both from unnecessary external constraint and internal deliberation, and toward full human emergence, autonomy, and actualization" (p. 17).

Epilogue

We believe that proponents of various philosophic camps generally are more concerned with finding better ways of doing what they are already doing than with raising questions as to why it is that they do what they do. We suggest that those conducting and reporting teaching effectiveness research expend some effort in examining the basic assumptions underpinning their research questions. The hoped-for result of this effort would be that educators demonstrate a higher level of sophistication in becoming more sensitive and aware of hidden or silent biases involved in recommendations and/or pressure to subscribe to current fads and trends resulting from teaching effectiveness research.

References

Anderson, L. M., Evertson, C. M., & Brophy, J. R. (1979). An experimental study of effective teaching in first-grade reading groups. Elementary School Journal, 79, 193-223.

Anderson, G., & Walberg, H. (1967). Classroom climate and group learning. (ERIC Document Reproduction Service No. ED 015 156)

Apple, M. W. (1982). Curriculum form and the logic of technical control: Building the possessive individual. In M. W. Apple (Ed.), Cultural and economic reproduction in education: Essays on class, ideology, and the state (pp. 247-274). London: Routledge & Kegan Paul, Ltd.

Aspy, D., & Roebuck, F. (1980). Teacher education: A response to Watt's response to Combs. Educational Leadership, 37, 507-510.

Aspy, D., & Roebuck, F. (1982). Affective education: Sound investment. Educational Leadership, 39, 488-494.

Aspy, D., & Roebuck, F. (1983). Our research and our findings. In C. R. Rogers, Freedom to learn for the 80's. Columbus, OH: Charles E. Merrill.

Braun, C. (1973). Johnny reads the cues: Teacher expectation. The Reading Teacher, 26, 704-712.

Brophy, J. E. (1979). Teacher behavior and its effects. Journal of Educational Psychology, 71, 733-750.

Brophy, J. E., & Good, T. L. (1970). Teachers' communication of differential expectations for children's classroom performance: Some behavioral data. Journal of Educational Psychology, 61, 365-374.

Brown, B. B. (1968). The experimental mind in education. New York: Harper & Row.

Bruner, J. S. (1958). Social psychology and perception. In E. E. Maccaby, T. M. Newcomb, & E. L. Hartley (Eds.), Readings in social psychology (pp. 101-122). New York: Holt, Rinehart & Winston.

Castle, K. (1982). Developmental stages of teaching. Unpublished manuscript, Oklahoma State University, College of Education, Stillwater, OK 74078.

Childress, B., & Dobson, R. L. (1973). Elementary teachers' philosophies of human nature and students' perceptions of the elementary school. Journal of the Student Personnel Association for Teacher Education, 11, 153-161.

Coker, H., Medley, D. M., & Soar, R. S. (1980). How valid are expert opinions about effective teaching? Phi Delta Kappan, 62, 131-134.

Combs, A. W. (1962). Perceiving, behaving, becoming. Washington DC: Association of Supervision and Curriculum Development.

Combs, A. W. (Ed.) (1969). Florida studies in the helping professions. Social Science Monograph, (Report No. 37). Gainesville: University of Florida Press.

Combs, A.W. (1982). A personal approach to training: Teaching beliefs that make a difference. Boston: Allyn & Bacon.

Davidson, H., & Lang, G. (1960). Children's perceptions of their teachers' feelings toward them related to self-perception, school achievement, and behavior. Journal of Experimental Education, 30, 116-20.

Deal, M., Dobson, R. L., & Dobson, J. E. (1982). Education graduate students' philosophies of human nature, levels of moral reasoning, and pupil control ideology. Teaching Learning Review, 3, 11-14.

Dewey, J. (1964). The continuum of ends-means. In R. Archanabault (Ed.), John Dewey on education (pp. 97-107). Chicago: University of Chicago Press. (Originally published, 1910)

Dieken, E. H., & Fox, R. B. (1973). Self-perception of teachers and their verbal behavior in the classroom. Educational Leadership, 30, 445-449.

Dobson, R. L., Hopkins, S., & Elsom, B. (1973). Elementary teachers' philosophies of human nature and nonverbal communication patterns. Journal of the Student Personnel Association for Teacher Education, 11, 98-101.

Dobson, R. L., Sewell, R., & Shelton, J. E. (1974). The congruency of verbal and nonverbal behavior of elementary school teachers with differing beliefs about the nature of man. Journal of the Student Association for Teacher Education, 12, 157-164.

Dobson, J. E., Grey, B., & Dobson, R. L., (1979, November). The effects of teacher-counselor consultation on the sociometric status and achievement of elementary school children. Resources in Education, ED 172103.

Eisner, E. (1983). The art and craft of teaching. Educational Leadership, 40, 4-14.

Fisher, C., Mariave, R., & Filby, N. (1979). Improving teaching by increasing academic learning time. Educational Leadership, 37, 52-54.

Freire, P. (1981). The adult literacy process as cultural action for freedom. In J. R. Snarey, F. Epstein, C. Sienkiewicz, & P. Zodhiates (Eds.), Conflict and continuity: A history of ideas on social equality and human development (pp. 87-115). (Reprint Series, No. 15), Boston: Harvard Educational Review.

Getzels, J. H., & Jackson, P. W. (1963). The teacher's personality and characteristics. In N. L. Gage (Ed.), Handbook of research on teaching (pp. 506-582). Chicago: University of Chicago Press.

Good, T. (1979). Teacher effectiveness in the elementary school: What we know about it now. Journal of Teacher Education, 30, 52-64.

Good, T., Biddle, B., & Brophy, J. (1975). Teachers make a difference. New York: Holt, Rinehart & Winston.

Hamachek, D. (1969). Characteristics of good teachers and implications for teacher education. Phi Delta Kappan, 50, 341-344.

Joyce, B., & Weil, M. (1980). Models of teaching (2nd ed.). Englewood Cliffs, NJ: Prentice-Hall.

Katz, L. (1977). Teachers' developmental stages. Talks with teachers. Washington DC: National Association for the Education of Young Children.

Kelley, E. C., & Rasey, M. I. (1952). Education and the nature of man. New York: Harper.

Kessinger, J. P. (1980). Perceptual base line system: An alternative strategy for teacher inservice education. (Doctoral dissertation, Oklahoma State University, 1979). Dissertation Abstracts International, 40, 4385A-4386A.

Land, G. (1973). Grow or die. New York: Random House.

Macdonald, J. (1975). The quality of everyday life in schools. In J. B. Macdonald & E. Zaret (Eds.), Schools in search of meaning (pp. 78-94). Washington, DC: Association for Supervision and Curriculum Development.

Marshall, J. P. (1973). The teacher and his philosophy. Lincoln Nebraska: Professional Educators Publication.

Mason, R. (1967). A comparative study of the relationships between seminary students and counselor trainees in their perceptions of human nature and tendencies toward authoritarianism. (Doctoral dissertation, University of Georgia, 1966). Dissertation Abstracts International, 27, 3292A. (University Microfilms No. 67-3570)

Medley, D. M. (1982). Teacher effectiveness. In H. E. Mitzel (Ed.), Encyclopedia of educational research (pp. 1894-1903). New York: Free Press.

Mendoza, S. M., Good, T. L., & Brophy, J. E. (1971, April). The communication of teacher expectancies in a junior high school. Paper presented at the meeting of the American Educational Research Association, New York.

Morris, V. C. (1966). Philosophy and educational development. Boston: Houghton Mifflin.

Peters, R. S. (1977). Must an education have an aim? In A. Bellack & H. Kliebard (Eds.), Curriculum and evaluation (pp. 123-130). Berkeley: McCutchan.

Peterson, P. (1979). Direct instruction: Effective for what and for whom? Educational Leadership, 37, 46-48.

Raskow, E., Airasian, R., & Madaus, G. (1978). Assessing school and program effectiveness: Estimating teacher level effects. Journal of Educational Measurement, 15, 15-21.

Rogers, C. R. (1983). Freedom to learn for the 80's. Columbus, OH: Charles E. Merrill.

Rosenshine, B. (1976). Classroom instruction. In N. L. Gage (Ed.), The psychology of teaching methods: Seventy-fifth yearbook of the national society for the study of education (pp. 335-370). Chicago: University of Chicago Press.

Rosenthal, R., & Jacobson, L. (1968). Pygmalion in the classroom. New York: Holt, Rinehart & Winston.

Russell, D. H., & Fea, H. R. (1963). Research on teaching reading. In N. L. Gage (Ed.), Handbook for research on teaching (pp. 865-928). Chicago: University of Chicago Press.

Ryan, K., & Phillips, D. H. (1982). Teacher characteristics. In H. E. Mitzel (Ed.), Encyclopedia of educational research (pp. 1869-1876). New York: Free Press.

Seay, N. L. (1982). Teacher concerns questionnaire as a measure of teachers' developmental stages. Unpublished master's thesis. Oklahoma State University, Stillwater.

Shallcross, D. J. (1979, November). Transformational theory as a motivation toward inservice education. Paper presented at the meeting of National Council of States on Inservice Education Convention, Hollywood, FL.

Sinclair, R. L. (1968). Elementary school educational environment: Measurement of selected variables of environmental press. Dissertation Abstracts International, 29, 3048A. (University Microfilms No. 69-5252)

Snow, R. E. (1969). Unfinished pygmalion. Contemporary Psychology, 14, 197-199.

Thorndike, R. L. (1968). Review of R. Rosenthal and L. Jacobson, Pygmalion in the classroom. American Educational Research Journal, 5, 708-711.

Tom, A. R. (1977). Critique of performance based teacher education. Educational Forum, 42, 77-87.

Weller, R. H. (Ed.) (1977). Humanistic education. Berkeley: McCutchan.

West, P. T. (1972). Self actualization resolving the individual-organization conflict. Clearing House, 47, 249-252.

Wiles, J., & Bondi, J. (1979). Curriculum development: A guide to practice. Columbus, OH: Charles E. Merrill.

Withall, J., & Lewis W. W. (1963). Social Interation in the classroom. In N. L. Gage (Ed.), Handbook of Research on Teaching (pp. 683-714). Chicago: University of Chicago Press.

Wright, D. P. (1980). Teachers' educational beliefs. A Study of Schooling (Tech. Rep. No. 14). Los Angeles: University of California.

Wrightsman, L. S. (1964). Measurements of philosopohies of human nature. Psychological Reports, 14, 743-75.

Wrightsman, L. S. (1974). Assumptions about human nature: A social-psychological approach. Monterey, CA: Brooks/Cole.

Zeichner, K. M. (1979a, February). The dialectics of teacher socialization. Paper presented at the meeting of the Association of Teacher Educators, Orlando, FL.

Zeichner, K. M. (1979b, April). Reflective teaching and field-based experience in teacher education. Paper presented at the meeting of the American Educational Research Association, San Francisco.

Zeichner, K. M. (1980, February). The student-teaching seminar: A vehicle for the development of reflective teachers. Paper presented at the meeting of the Association of Teacher Educators, Washington, DC.

Zeichner, K. M. (1981, February). Ethical problems in 'personalizing' instruction during the student teaching experience. Paper presented at the meeting of the Association of Teacher Experience, Dallas.

SECTION IV

ALTERNATIVES TO CONSIDER

A paradox exists in today's schools. Modern school educators are generally more sophisticated than their counterparts of a decade ago. However, many children still encounter learning difficulties similar to those of the past. There is an established trend toward attempting to minimize and/or resolve instructional difficulties brought about by human variability among children through such devices as the non-graded school, individually prescribed instruction, differentiated staffing, computer assisted instruction, and other grand organizational or instructional schemes. In spite of organizational and instructional manipulation, the school experience for some children still remains dismal, often resulting in failure.

Throughout this book we have alluded to the premise that a different focus is needed in education. An attempt to facilitate the optimal growth and development of each individual child is long overdue. We submit that a need exists for schools to establish as top priority how children learn and what their feelings are concerning what they learn. In other words, perhaps equal time should be given to what children are and could be as to what they should be. Such an endeavor in schools would necessitate the creation of a school culture in which learning flourishes primarily because of internal student motivation rather than externally initiated stimuli.

Does the school encourage both teachers and students to be themselves? Are teachers and students valued for their individuality and autonomy? Is independence sought? Is personal meaning prized over accumulation and reiteration of facts?

We believe schools should be places of learning where children and teachers are challenged yet comfortable. This means that youngsters and teachers greet each day with enthusiasm and demonstrate eagerness instead of reluctance at being "in school." We also profess that children should be provided with school programs responsive to their needs and interests. In attempting to realize children's needs, teachers must facilitate the gaining of knowledge and also attempt to encourage children in discovering their own personal meanings of the knowledge.

In establishing person-centered schools, educators are confronted with the task of developing a curriculum in which function controls structure as opposed to structure dictating function. Essentially, this means taking into account the nature of children and developing instructional programs which enhance rather than stifle growth and development. If children are naturally curious and want to know about themselves and their environment, why are educators still preoccupied with the concept of motivation and why are children confronted with failure, learning disabilities, remediation, and the like? It may be that schools do not have control over the entire environment affecting the child's learning potential, but it safely can be assumed that the school has enough influence on this corner of the child's universe to accept some responsibility for causal factors which ultimately influence his/her successes and failures.

Chapter 6 presents a rationale for schools which encourages congruency between individual teachers' educational beliefs and practices. Chapter 7 presents and explains a process definition of curriculum—a model beginning with human existence. This section ends with Chapter 8, a description of an inservice model focusing on humans, children, youth, and teachers.

Since teachers are confronted with multiple choices for schooling the young, it is vital that they understand their own values and beliefs about schooling. This chapter (a) presents an argument for teacher beliefs-practice congruency, (b) establishes possible reasons why congruency is neglected, and (c) discusses dialogue as a process for arriving at congruency.

CHAPTER 6

TEACHER BELIEFS-PRACTICE CONGRUENCY*

> There is no such thing as
> truth or reality for a
> living human being except
> as he participates in it, is
> conscious of it, and has
> some relationship to it.

—Rollo May

There are, within the ranks of educators, those who have chosen to remain permanently immature. By this we mean there are those who refuse to assume responsibility for their teaching actions and alternately assign this project to others. What teachers choose to do to, for, or with students does not occur in a vacuum. There is no such thing as value neutral action; teaching practices, whether consciously or unconsciously chosen, are expressions of beliefs held by the teacher.

As it is reasonable to expect politicians' actions to be guided by their political philosophies (or at least some discernible belief system), it is reasonable to expect teachers to be guided by educational philosophies or at least some close facsimile (Tranel, 1981). Marshall (1973) suggests that teachers cannot achieve the objectives of refining and improving their craft until they are fairly certain of their personal value orientations, the purpose and objectives that grow out of their values, and a set of criteria anchored in something deeper than the convenience of the moment, or a simple hunch. Shallcross (1979) and Katz (1977) in their models of professional development of teachers suggest that mature professionals are guided in their actions by a set of internalized personal beliefs.

In this chapter we argue that humans are the inventors or creators of their own belief systems and that belief systems are beacons which guide daily lives and ultimately affect the degree to which humans experience themselves as well as others. To succumb to an imposed reality is to experience the loss or prostitution of personal beliefs, resulting in alienation from self as well as others, thus leading to role behavior which may be incongruent.

Shaw (1975) defines congruence as organic harmony between one's authentic self and one's lifework. Aspy and Roebuck (1977, p. 6) state

*This chapter first appeared as an article which we authored for Viewpoints in Teaching and Learning, 57(1) (Winter 1983), 20-27. Copyright 1983 VTL.

that congruence means genuiness, "...the degree to which an individual's words and actions accurately reflect her or his own feelings and attitudes."

We believe that any real improvement in schooling will occur only when teachers are experiencing beliefs-practice congruency. To present this argument we (a) attempt to construct a rationale for teacher beliefs-practice congruency, (b) identify possible reasons why congruency, as an important concept, is neglected in teacher effectiveness literature, and (c) present a discussion of dialogue as a process for arriving at congruency.

Why Be Congruent?

Teachers' educational beliefs have been extensively studied by researchers in recent years. Although this chapter is not a review of previous research, it seems appropriate to mention earlier findings which support the contention that relatively few teachers have developed internally consistent philosophies (Brown, 1968; Childress & Dobson, 1973; Davis, Dobson, & Shelton, 1973; Deal, Dobson, & Dobson, 1982; Dobson, Goldenberg, & Elsom, 1972; Dobson, Hopkins, & Elsom, 1973; Dobson, Sewell, & Shelton, 1974; Kessinger, 1980; Wright, 1980).

There is ample evidence to suggest that classroom teachers seldom adopt teaching models in accordance with their professed beliefs. Marshall (1973) contends that teachers proceed with eclectic approaches composed of bits of data from diverse psychological and philosophical camps.

Considering this state of the art, it seems that a more systematic treatment of teacher beliefs-practice congruency relative to curriculum and instruction would be useful. A search of the literature (Dobson, Dobson, & Koetting, 1982) reveals that the bulk of research on teaching effectiveness during the past decade has been done without any reference to underlying philosophical assumptions.

Teaching practice without the support provided by a well-developed philosophy (set of beliefs) proceeds at random, blindly. Teaching without purpose becomes mere activity to "get things done" with little consideration of means-ends compatibility. Our culture seems to encourage a pragmatic approach toward almost every activity. Teachers are part of the culture and tend to reject philosophy and approach each task without concern for keeping their beliefs and practices consistent and harmonious.

Wiles and Bondi (1979) suggest that educational philosophies form the heart of purposeful activity. They state that since teachers are confronted with multiple choices for schooling the young, it is vital that teachers understand their personal values and beliefs about schooling.

Why is Congruency Neglected?

To be able to attend to all the complexities associated with any "why" questions is impossible. However, to refuse to attend to a question will not wish it away. The following discussion presents several possible reasons why congruency is neglected.

Time Consumption. To pursue questions of "What is good?", "What is true?", and "What is real?" requires time, study, reflection, and hopefully some form of dialogue with others. Due to the nature of schooling, the "hustle-bustle" of accomplishing the job and improving upon it while doing so, teachers simply are not given sufficient time or encouragement to think through beliefs and clarify values (self-introspection). Only when a faculty, through honest dialogue (patient discussion and listening), develop a shared philosophy have they a foundation from which to examine variables such as curriculum, organization, instruction, evaluation, school mission, and society. An identified and hopefully shared set of beliefs enables a faculty to order priorities, establish goals, identify activities, analyze conflicting proposals, and convert controversy into meaningful school experiences.

Values Seen as Abstractions. The importance of values in educational decision making can be demonstrated by value words such as goals, objectives, adequacy, greatest importance, and priorities. Abstractness is assigned to values, and too often teachers refuse to deal with them. Values are not so abstract nor elusive that teachers cannot grasp their place in the schooling process. Teachers cannot afford to continue to ignore the impact of values in planning and decision making. Declared value systems provide guidelines for planning the future. To attempt to forecast, predict, or engage in long-range planning while ignoring the value bases of those involved in and affected by the decisions is to plan for failure.

We do not intend to imply that values are totally neglected in educational planning. Most school policy manuals set forth noble goals for human activity. However, we submit that this aspect is treated in a casual manner. Teachers seem to assume that everyone knows the values so there is no point in wasting time with exploration. What often happens is that what everyone seems to know, no one knows.

Role Access. It is immoral to expect teachers to continue to leave their "persons" outside the door as they enter the classroom. Nor can teachers be the epitome of neutrality as they assume the role of teacher. (Teacher role is defined as a norm with concomitant skill criteria which all are expected to perform.)

To recapitulate what we stated in Chapter 4, past attempts at improving teaching performance can be labeled "role access." Improvement is seen as increasing the number of role behaviors to which teachers have access and can perform successfully. This activity results in teachers exchanging one set of role behaviors for another set which have been decreed as appropriate by those in authority. The person in the process may or may not have changed. The procedure is based on the assumption that those in superordinate positions know more than do those in subordinate positions about what constitutes good teaching. Evidence simply does not exist to lend credibility to this assumption.

Technical Rationale. There have been cogent analyses at the theoretical/conceptual level examining technical rationale and how this notion, whether consciously or unconsciously, has affected thought within the field of curriculum and instruction (Apple, 1975; Giroux, Penna, & Pinar, 1981; Kliebard, 1975; Koetting, 1980). Technical rationale has become a reductionist view of a complex process; namely, education, wherein simplistic explanations of input/output become distorted views of scientific method applied to curriculum and instruction theory and design. Examples are systems theory, competency-based teacher education, behavior objectives movement, and instructional design. There has been a preoccupation with means-end thinking, resulting in an overwhelming positivistic attitude. As we stated in the previous chapter, this positivistic attitude, when transferred to instructional activities, views teaching, the inseparable companion of curriculum effort, as a science and a technology with identifiable, observable skills which are considered to be the "practice" of teaching. Again, while we admit there are certain teaching skills which can be taught and measured, we reject the idea that teaching is fundamentally comprised of the right mix of techniques, methods, and skills.

In any event, contemporary concern with teaching, theory and practice, reflects almost completely a technological rationale. As a result of the field becoming an increasingly highly skilled technology with a primary emphasis on method, teachers have been encouraged to restrict their focus on areas amenable to this technology. As Apple (1979) contends, the prevailing interest is to separate value from fact. The pseudo-scientist's perspective is a value-free posture as opposed to one which is value-laden.

Congruency Through Dialogue

We have argued that a need exists for teachers who develop, plan, and implement school curricula and instructional programs to seriously consider the philosophical implications of those variables they manipulate to affect learning within the classroom. A case has been presented which suggests that a unifying structure is lacking which entertains the role of philosophy (values and beliefs) in guiding the development, planning, and implementation of classroom practice and the school program. A need for more systematic treatment of philosophical beliefs as they relate to classroom practice has been established. In light of this condition, Greene (1973, p. 6) suggests if teachers want to be themselves and achieve something meaningful in the world then they should subscribe to a proposal "...which is nothing more than to think what we are doing."

Beliefs and practices in education revolve around three main philosophical camps or schools of thought. These are Essentialism, Experimentalism, and Existentialism, with their respective counterparts represented in three psychological movements labeled Behaviorism, Cognitivism, and Humanism. Each of the camps deals with questions relative to the following variables: (a) The nature of humans; (b) the nature of learning; (c) the nature of knowledge; (d) the nature of society; (e) the purposes of schooling; (f) the nature of curriculum; (g) the nature of instructional behavior; and (h) the nature of evaluation.

The preceding philosophical camps and educational variables are proposed as tentative content amenable to a dialogical process. Freire (1981) contends that in a dialogical process, the "common sense" perception of reality and the person's questioning of reality are subject to critical analysis. Freire calls this the decodification of reality.

A similar view of dialogue as a process of denouncing encapsulating forces operating upon the individual is discussed by Pritzkau (1970). For him, dialogue is:

Conversation between two or more persons in which each transcends solitude and accepts his aloneness and that of the other person, thereby seeking a form of transaction which maintains the maximum freedom of each.... This means that the individual has opened himself to receive messages from others as well as all types of media.... (pp. 11-12)

Zais (1976) contends that educators do not reach the level of dialogue. He states, "At its best, discussion is exchange of views, debate, or clarification. At its worst, it is merely role playing. In any case, it is rarely self-critical" (p. 241). True dialogue is achieved with the purpose of clarifying one's personal beliefs, the searching for more complete structures of meaning.

The search for congruence is an active process by individual teachers which involves reflection on personal knowledge, educational theory, and educational practices. The method we propose for beginning the search for beliefs-practice congruency is the awakening of consciousness through dialogue. We stated in Chapter I that according to Freire (1981), an educational experience which places dialogue at its center starts the dialogical process. "It is a questioning process about possible 'thematic universes' expressing the relationship of the persons involved in dialogue with the world" (p. 86).

In order for teachers to act upon their beliefs and current practices, they need to realize that both constitute moments of the same process, that values immersed in beliefs and practices is reality which, for the existentialist, is not a fixed entity--something given. Teachers need to feel free in order to act upon their realities, introducing change gradually,

91

contingent to their being. Freire (1981, p. 62) expresses, "Reality is really a process, undergoing constant transformation."

A dialogical situation serves the purpose of clarifying teachers' thoughts with one another; in this process they no longer learn in isolation, but rather in a world context with their peers. This is not only a process involving the cognition of a given situation, but of reconsidering personal ways of approaching the situation under study. When teachers reflect on their being through the building of new structures of meanings, they become aware they are building themselves in the process.

In the dialogical process of searching for beliefs-practice congruency, teachers can become aware of the limitations hindering harmony. From subsequent elaboration of meanings they expose their newly gained critical understanding which, in Freire's (1981) thesis, corresponds to a dual process of denunciation and annunciation discussed in Chapter I.

Difficulties will be met in the process of bringing about beliefs-practice congruency. As teachers bring beliefs and practices together through thought and action to a level of critical awareness, contradictions arise. The obstacles met are not impediments to action but "limit situations" (Freire, 1981). Limit situations can give origin to new meaningful structures since the limitations are felt by the participants involved in critical dialogue. An overcoming of limit situations results in the posing of new problems by those involved and corresponds to what Freire (1981) calls the "investigation of thematics" which

> ...involves the investigation of the people's thinking - which occurs only in and among men together seeking out reality. I cannot think FOR OTHERS, nor can OTHERS, think FOR ME. Even if the thinking is...naive, it is only as they rethink their assumptions in action that they can change. Producing and acting upon their own ideas - not consuming those of others - must constitute that process. (p. 100)

Through dialogue teachers can overcome limit situations which result in lack of harmony between what they profess and what they actually practice.

Summary

Some readers may believe the thesis of this chapter, the belief that teachers will function more effectively when they are experiencing beliefs-practice congruency, is hopelessly unrealistic and idealistic. We have argued the opposite. To continue to ignore values and beliefs under the disguise of a pseudo-scientific notion of "value-neutrality" is to continue in a naive and simplistic direction resulting in the creation and perpetuation of half-truths relative to the teaching experience.

One who is even casually acquainted with the literature of teaching effectiveness/teacher competency research readily recognizes that the current focus is on finding better ways of doing what is already being done rather than on raising critical questions as to why we do what we do. The emphasis has been on improving rather than understanding the teacher-learning experience. It seems apparent that researchers might well afford to spend time and effort examining the philosophic roots of basic assumptions underpinning their research efforts.

Evidence seems to authenticate the posture that issues and problems related to the process of teaching are consequences of divided perceptions of reality and values. As a result, the critical issues must be entertained philosophically and not be left solely to the ploy of dispassionate pragmatists. If this implies that teachers be given greater opportunity for understanding basic systems of philosophy and the relationships connecting the philosophic positions with educational points of view, and, in turn, the relationship of these points of view to decisions they make regarding classroom methods and procedures, then so be it. This chapter has attempted to focus upon this need.

References

Apple, M. W. (1975). Scientific interests and the nature of educational institutions. In W. Pinar (Ed.), Curriculum theorizing: The reconceptualists (pp. 120-130). Berkeley: McCutchan.

Apple, M. (1979). Ideology and curriculum. London: Routledge & Kegan Paul, Ltd.

Aspy, D., & Roebuck, F. (1977). Kids don't learn from people they don't like. Amherst, MA: Human Resources Development Press.

Brown, B. B. (1968). The experimental mind in education. New York: Harper & Row.

Childress, B., & Dobson, R. L. (1973). Elementary teachers' philosophies of human nature and students' perceptions of the elementary school. Journal of the Student Personnel Association for Teacher Education, 11, 153-161.

Davis, G., Dobson, R. L., & Shelton, J. E. (1973). Nonverbal behavior of first grade teachers in different socioeconomic level elementary schools. Journal of the Student Personnel Association for Teacher Education, 11, 76-80.

Deal, M., Dobson, R. L., & Dobson, J. E. (1982). Education graduate students' philosophies of human nature, levels of moral reasoning and pupil control ideology. Teaching Learning Review, 3, 11-14.

Dobson, R. L., Goldenberg, R., & Elsom, B. (1972). Pupil control ideology and teacher influence in the classroom. Journal of Educational Research, 67, 76-80.

Dobson, R. L., Hopkins, S., & Elsom, B. (1973). Elementary teachers' philosophies of human nature and nonverbal communication patterns. Journal of the Student Personal Association for Teacher Education, 11, 98-101.

Dobson, R. L., Sewell, R., & Shelton, J. E. (1974). The congruency of verbal and nonverbal behavior of elementary school teachers with differing beliefs about the nature of man. Journal of the Student Personnel Association for Teacher Education, 12, 157-164.

Dobson, R. L., Dobson, J. E., & Koetting, J. R. (1982). The language of teaching effectiveness and teacher competency research. Viewpoints in Teaching and Learning, 58(2), 23-33.

94

Freire, P. (1981). The adult literacy process as cultural action for freedom. In J. R. Snarey, F. Epstein, C. Sienkiewicz, & P. Zodhiates (Eds.), Conflict and continuity: A history of ideas on social equality and human development (pp. 87-115). (Reprint Series No. 15). Boston: Harvard Educational Review.

Giroux, H., Penna, A. N., & Pinar, W. F. (Eds.). (1981). Curriculum and instruction: Alternatives in education. Berkeley: McCutchan.

Greene, M. (1973). Teacher as stranger. Belmont, CA: Wadsworth.

Katz, L. (1977). Talks with teachers. Washington, DC: National Association for the Education of Young Children.

Kessinger, J. P. (1980). Perceptual base line system: An alternative strategy for teacher inservice education. (Doctoral dissertation, Oklahoma State University, 1979.) Dissertation Abstracts International, 40, 4385A-4386A.

Kliebard, H. (1975). Bureaucracy and curriculum theory. In W. Pinar (Ed.), Curriculum theorizing: The reconceptualists (pp. 51-69). Berkeley: McCutchan.

Koetting, J. R. (1980). Towards a theory of knowledge and human interests, educational technology and emancipatory education: A preliminary theoretical investigation and critique. (Doctoral Dissertation, University of Wisconsin-Madison, 1979.) Dissertation Abstracts International, 40, 6118A.

Marshall, J. P. (1973). The teacher and his philosophy. Lincoln, NE: Professional Educators Publication.

May, R. (1969). Love and will. New York: W. W. Norton.

Pritzkau, P. F. (1970). On education for the authentic. New York: Thomas J. Crowell.

Shallcross, D. J. (1979, November). Transformational theory and creative decision-making as bases for planning inservice programs. Paper presented at the National Council of States on Inservice Education Convention, Hollywood, FL.

Shaw, F. (1975). Congruence. In W. Pinar (Ed.), Curriculum theorizing: The reconceptualists (pp. 445-452). Berkeley: McCutchan.

Tranel, D. (1981). A lesson from physicists. Personnal and Guidance Journal, 59, 425-429.

Wiles, J., & Bondi, J. (1979). Curriculum development: A guide to practice. Columbus, OH: Charles E. Merrill.

Wright, D. P. (1980). Teachers' educational beliefs. A study of schooling (Tech. Rep. No. 14). Los Angeles: University of California.

Zais, R. S. (1976). Curriculum: Principles and foundations. New York: Harper & Row.

In this chapter we propose a definition/model of curriculum which presents a view of humans and then proceeds to translate this view into the curriculum function. Essentially, this means taking into account the essence of children and developing a curriculum which facilitates human growth and development. Our purpose is to revitalize the significance of the child as a human, an integral consideration in the curriculum adventure.

CHAPTER 7

TOWARD A PROCESS DEFINITION OF CURRICULUM: HUMAN EXISTENCE TO FORMATIVE EVALUATION*

Although curriculum had its beginning as a field of study approximately one-half century ago, theorists still have not arrived at consensus on what constitutes a standard definition/model. Early on, curriculum was viewed as a package of universal knowledge to be delivered to the learner; linear relationships between ends and means were stressed (Bobbitt, 1918/1971; Charters, 1923; Johnson, 1967; Smith, Stanley, & Shores, 1957; Tyler, 1974). This perspective resulted in curriculum being viewed as a product comprised of the right mix of content, objectives, scope, sequence, structure, activities, and evaluation. All of this could be packaged and delivered to the learner.

More recently there has emerged a group of theorists who have presented a cogent analysis which concludes that this perspective of curriculum has resulted in a technical rationale (Apple, 1975; Eisner, 1979; Giroux, Penna, & Pinar, 1981; Kliebard, 1975; Macdonald, 1975; Pinar, 1975). Theorists from this camp argue that technical rationale (man as machine metaphor) is a reductionist view of a complex process (education) wherein simplistic explanations of input (student as raw material) and output (student as product) have become a distorted view of the scientific method applied to curriculum theory and design. There has been a preoccupation with end-means thinking resulting in an overwhelming positivistic attitude regarding expressions of curriculum workers.

Discussions relative to curriculum debate must opt for a logically coherent philosophy. As Roberts (1976, p. 321) succinctly states, "It is impossible to practice the ideas of Skinner and Chomsky simultaneously." As suggested in Chapter 6, we would expect politicians' actions to be guided by their political philosophies, or at least by some discernible belief system. We would further add it is not unreasonable to expect curriculum theorists and workers to be guided by educational philosophies or at least some close facsimile.

Definitions/models of curriculum in and of themselves are neither good nor bad, right nor wrong. It is the interpretation of these definitions/models into human actions, not necessarily the definitions/models themselves, that in the end pose a threat. A definition/model of a phenomenon is not the phenomenon itself, but merely a representation. Edelman (1973) established that language used by theorists tends to establish their reality and subtly justify their

*This chapter is a revised version of our article which first appeared in The Journal of Humanistic Education, 7 (Spring, 1983), 37-40. Copyright 1983 JHE.

actions. This function is not unique to any particular philosophic camp. The power of language to shape and freeze reality is a notion worthy of curriculum workers' attention.

"Establishment" definitions/models of curriculum tend to support a value neutral position. As stated earlier, curriculum is seen as a package of universal content to be delivered to the student. The nature of the package and the mode of delivery reflect certain beliefs about humans. The delivery of the curriculum package determines the functions necessary for the student to perform in order to be educated (terminate school). In this case, structure (the curriculum package) determines function (the way the student will act). This raises questions for curriculum theorists/workers. Should structure determine function? Should function determine structure? Should there be a reciprocal arrangement? In other words, should the curriculum serve to define and shape children into what they should be, or should curriculum be an educational expression of the way children are?

In this chapter we propose a definition/model of curriculum which presents a view of humans and then proceeds to translate this view into the curriculum function. Essentially, this means taking into account the nature of children and developing a curriculum which facilitates human growth and development. Our purpose is to revitalize the significance of the child as a human in the curriculum adventure.

In order to fulfill our proposal, we (a) suggest a set of criteria for a process definition/model of curriculum, (b) present assumptions for a process/definition model, (c) submit a process/definition model, and finally, (d) present a utilitarian function of the definition/model.

Borrowing from the work of Combs (1974), we propose the following criteria for a process definition of curriculum. Curriculum must be:

1. Capable of dealing with the internal life of persons-- feelings, values, and the like. A process definition of curriculum therefore will go beyond surface reality of performance and deal with personal knowledge/meaning, critical thinking, and analysis, and the value-base for decision making;

2. Orderly in its progression, i.e., systematic in its analyses of issues and problems;

3. Applicable to the problems of the individual case, a guide to action (a process definition of curriculum will, by necessity, go beyond prepackaged materials and content to an examination of individual life-circumstances); and

4. Dynamic and immediate rather than descriptive. A process definition cannot be absolute and final since it responds to an ongoing understanding of the human condition.

Assumptions for a Process Definition

Any attempt to order reality, an aspect of theory building, must, by necessity, begin with assumptions relative to the phenomenon under investigation. These assumptions, in turn, serve as criteria for assessing the theory endeavor. Our proposed definition/model of curriculum has as its focal point the essence of children and their activity. The assumptions are:

1. Humans have the potential for becoming whomever they choose.

2. Humans create their own unique being and existence through choices made from among the alternatives presented by their environment, thus the uniqueness of individuals.

3. Knowledge exists only within the individual and is a synthesization of information. Knowledge is a model created by the individual that makes sense of encounters with external conditions in the environment.

4. Through the process of selection and/or valuing, humans create their own values. Associated with their values are certain consequences which can be either positive or negative in nature. Thus, associated with the freedom to choose is the responsibility to one's self to live with the consequences. Without the freedom-responsibility association there is neither self-order nor a vehicle for assimilating beliefs and actions into a positive force. This is the human condition of learning.

5. Humans are more than can ever be known about them. Humans are best described as total entities.

6. Humans are inherently inclined to be good rather than destructive.

Process Definition of Curriculum

As reflected in the preceding assumptions, a particular philosophical perspective of humans is inherent in a process definition of curriculum. Most definitions of curriculum are stated as product definitions; a linear relationship between ends and means is stressed. It can be argued that

101

operational definitions are often more restrictive than descriptive. Conversely, a process definition of curriculum (our preference) emphasizes that ends or objectives are outcomes of activity which give meaning to and redirect future activity. This perspective becomes the cornerstone for advocating what children will do in daily practice in school. Thus, we submit that a process definition of curriculum is an attempted and ongoing definition of humans (children) translated into educational specifications. The definition, by its nature, encourages philosophic congruency between theory and practice. The definition meets the criteria established earlier in that the school experience is an extension of how the child is (a thinking, valuing human). It is orderly rather than chaotic in that systematic movement is encouraged from an identified perspective of humans to daily practice. It is applicable to the individual case in that it provides for a reciprocal arrangement between structure and function, thus allowing for the uniqueness of individuals. And finally, it is dynamic and immediate since a final definition of humans is not established, thus allowing for the incorporation of the unimagined and yet-to-be-discovered potential of humans.

A further explanation of the definition is provided through the presentation of a two-part model in Figures 2 and 3. Humans can be described in terms of existence, condition, and potential (ECP). These three dimensions are presented in the ECP submodel (Figure 2). Within each individual there is existence. This existence is composed of an interplay of certain aspects--such as needs, feelings, intellect, and the like--depicted in the model. The active expression of existence is the human condition. Flowing from the exchange of existence and condition is human potential.

An example from the ECP model which can be used to interpret humans is demonstrated by viewing Cell A in all three blocks. If inherent within human existence is freedom (A1), and if the human condition for actively expressing freedom is choice (A2), then the potential of responsibility (A3) is a reality. Another example is Cell E of feeling (E1), emotion (E2), and awareness (E3). The ECP model is an attempt to explain humans in their constant struggle to express potentials.

Identifying an educational process compatiable with the ECP submodel requires a second submodel which describes the purpose, experience, and formative evaluation (PEFE) of the school experience (see Figure 3). The potentials of humans, identified in the ECP model, reasonably become the purposes of schooling identified in the PEFE model. The design of educational experiences reflecting school purposes has as its derivation the human condition as established in the ECP model. The quality of the experiences (formative evaluation) can be ascertained by the degree to which the total experience has reflected and cultivated human existence. This is in keeping with the perspective that life is being-all-one-is as opposed to being shaped into something one is not, thus requiring an interplay between structure and function.

102

FORMATIVE EVALUATION

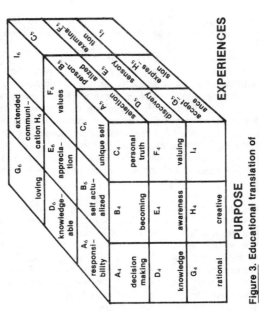

PURPOSE

Figure 3. Educational translation of humans: Purpose, experience, formative evaluation (PEFE).

EXPERIENCES

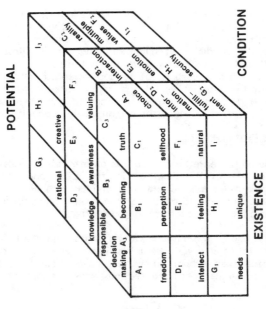

EXISTENCE

Figure 2. Definition/Model of humans: Existence, condition, potential (ECP).

CONDITION

POTENTIAL

103

In the final analysis, the ECP model attempts to define humans, and the PEFE model attempts to present an institutional (school) expression of humans: the purpose, experience, and formative evaluation of the schooling experience. Grahlman (1976) provides an in-depth discussion of the derivation and definitions of cells and interaction of the items contained within each of the cells in both submodels. The linkage between the two submodels becomes apparent upon realizing that the first consideration of the PEFE model, purpose of school, is identical to the final consideration of the ECP model, humans' ultimate potential. In other words, any educational expression of humans must of necessity begin with inherent potential. This potential should be the source of direction for determining curriculum and instruction experiences. The cells in the PEFE model culminate ultimately at the formative evaluation level.

Consider how the PEFE model works by viewing Cell A in each of the three elements. If becoming responsible decision makers is a potential of humans (Cell A3 of the ECP model), then helping them move toward this potential becomes a purpose of school (Cell A4 of the PEFE model). This being the case, then, it follows that for this purpose to be realized children must be provided the experience of selection (Cell A5) which is an educational translation of the human condition of choice (Cell A2). Formative evaluation (Cell A6) would be the level of responsibility children exhibit to themselves and others.

The Congruency of ECP and PEFE

Figure 4 represents a fusion of the models in order to further clarify the process. An example of the congruency of the two models can be demonstrated by viewing Cell G. If, through existence, humans have needs, and if the condition of humans allows for fulfillment of these needs, then it follows that they have the potential to become rational human beings. If one purpose of process-oriented curriculum is the development of the rational person, that is, one who does not do harm to self or others, and this person experiences acceptance, then the formative evaluation is the extent to which the person has the capacity to be loving.

The Utility of ECP and PEFE

The schema presented in Figure 5 is an attempt to assist the reader in identifying the utility inherent in the ECP and PEFE models. Educational objectives established by individual school systems can be filtered through the cells to check for congruence. In addition, the cells can be used as a framework for creating objectives.

Recently, one of the authors was serving as an outside facilitator in a school district that was designing implementation strategies for previously established school objectives. One objective--develop the ability to communicate ideas and feelings--was selected at random. As

THE EDUCATIONAL EXPERIENCE

| | HUMANS | | | |
	Existence	Condition	Potential-Purpose	Experience	Formative Evaluation
CELL A	Freedom	Choice	Responsible decision maker	Selection	Responsibility
B	Perception	Interaction	Becoming	Personalized	Self-actualized
C	Selfhood	Reality	Personal truth	Varied	Unique self
D	Intellect	Information	Knowledge	Discovery	Knowledgeable
E	Feeling	Emotional	Awareness	Sensory	Appreciation
F	Natural	Multiple values	Valuing	Examination	Personal values
G	Needs	Fulfillment	Rational	Acceptance	Loving
H	Unique	Security	Creative	Expression	Extended communication

Figure 4. The fusing of the ECP-PEFE Models: From theory to practice.

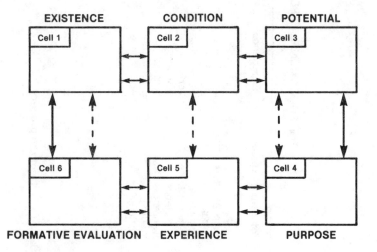

Figure 5. The utility of the ECP-PEFE models in checking educational objectives for congruency.

the staff attempted to identify communication as a potential of humans and place it in Cell 3, they experienced difficulty in identifying appropriate concepts to fit the remaining cells. They decided that to communicate was a human condition (Cell 2) and that a sense of community (Cell 3) was the realization of humans' potential. Thus, the cells were filled in the following manner (which resulted in the rewriting of the goal): Cell 1 Social, Cell 2 Communication, Cell 3 Community, Cell 4 Community, Cell 5 Acceptance, and Cell 6 Unity. The consensus of the staff was that the original goal was an expression of a limited view of humans, and the exercise resulted in a rewritten goal aimed at humans' potential.

Summary

Through the use of the two models and their fusion, we have attempted to bring some light to a very complex affair, process-oriented curriculum. The models are not intended to be final in nature but are presented as theoretical constructs to be considered by curriculum theorists/workers as they explore alternative curriculum definitions from both a practical and a theoretical perspective, if indeed such perspectives can be separated. The implementation of process-oriented curriculum necessitates internal consistency between an attempted definition of humans (the ECP model) and its translation into educational specifications (the PEFE model). Perhaps these two models can serve to facilitate this endeavor.

References

Apple, M. W. (1975). Scientific interests and the nature of educational institutions. In W. Pinar (Ed.), Curriculum theorizing: The reconceptualists (pp. 120-130). Berkeley: McCutchan.

Bobbitt, F. (1971). The curriculum. New York: Arno Press. (Original work published by Houghton Mifflin 1918).

Charters, W. W. (1923). Curriculum construction. New York: Macmillan.

Combs, A. W. (1974). Why the humanistic movement needs a perceptual psychology. Journal of the Association for the Study of Perception, 9 (4), 13-19.

Edelman, M. (1973). The political language of the helping professions. Unpublished manuscript, University of Wisconsin, Madison.

Eisner, E. (1979). The educational imagination. New York: Macmillan.

Giroux, H., Penna, A. N., & Pinar, W. F. (Eds.). (1981). Curriculum and instruction: Alternatives in education. Berkeley: McCutchan.

Grahlman, F. W. (1976). A heuristic model of accountability based on measurement of the human potential. (Doctoral dissertation, Oklahoma State University, 1975). Dissertation Abstracts International, 36, 7064A.

Johnson, M. (1967). Definitions and models in curriculum theory. Educational Theory, 17(9), 127-131.

Kliebard, H. (1975). Bureaucracy and curriculum theory. In W. Pinar (Ed.), Curriculum theorizing: The reconceptualists (pp. 51-69). Berkeley: McCutchan.

Macdonald, J. (1975). The quality of everyday life in schools. In J. Macdonald & E. Zaret (Eds.), Schools in search of meaning (pp. 78-94). Washington, DC: Association of Supervision and Curriculum Development.

Pinar, W. (Ed.). (1975). Curriculum theorizing: The reconceptualists. Berkeley: McCutchan.

Roberts, J. (1976). Freedom, the child, the teacher: A gap between ideas and actions. Theory Into Practice, 15(5), 319-325.

Smith B., Stanley, W., & Shores, J. (1957). Fundamentals of curriculum development. New York: Harcourt, Brace & World.

Tyler, R.   (1974).   <u>Basic principles of curriculum and instruction.</u>
Chicago: University of Chicago Press.

This chapter presents an inservice model based upon the premise that once teachers risk, build trust, and share with their peers, then they will feel free to risk, establish trust, and share in their interactions with students. We view this as an important ingredient in a school which encourages the potential of both students and teachers.

CHAPTER 8

RISK, TRUST, SHARE: AN INSERVICE MODEL
FOR HUMANISTIC EDUCATION*

Inservice education seems to be a sound means for creating humanistic teaching-learning conditions. It can facilitate personal and professional goals, continuity of faculty development efforts, activities with a purpose, and, ultimately, a way to translate philosophical perspectives into day-to-day educational practice.

Personal risk, trust, and sharing are necessary if a humanistic school atmosphere including fairness, honesty, order, stimulation, and freedom to do what one wishes as long as no harm is done to others (Goble 1970) is to become a realty. This inservice model is based upon the premise that once teachers risk, build trust, and share with their peers, then they will feel free to risk, establish trust, and share in their interactions with students. Risking even a small part of self in interactions with others is necessary to establish a trust base. Mutual trust with others is necessary to establish a trust base. We believe mutual trust is extremely important between and among teachers and students if schools are to provide environments which facilitate optimal human growth and development. Only when a trust base is established are teachers and students truly able to share in this living experience at school.

An examination of humanistic education suggests four major areas for focus and study: (a) theory/knowledge base; (b) basic beliefs and personal behaviors; (c) authentic communication; and (d) alternatives for implementation. In order to clarify the model, each of the inservice components or phases is presented separately and in sequence. The phases, however, do overlap. To implement this inservice education model, a variety of activities and strategies must be integrated. Specific suggestions for implementation according to each of the four components are proposed. However, resourceful educators will want to use additional activities or create original strategies. Suggested readings are included at the end of the chapter for use by the school staff as they engage in this cooperative effort.

Phase I: Theory/Knowledge Base

During this initial phase, inservice teachers read and discuss the underlying assumptions of humanistic education; humanism as a psychological base and existentialism as a philosophical base. Once the inherent concepts are understood, teachers derive, by consensus, the definition of humanistic education which they plan to implement in their

---

*This chapter is a revised version of our article which first appeared in The Humanist Educator, 24(1) (September, 1975), 32-39. Copyright 1975 THE.

school. Discussions with the professional staff must then focus on translating these concepts into educational practice.

Three possible strategies which inservice facilitators may consider when planning the meetings are brainstorming, comparing and contrasting open and closed educational processes, and incomplete sentences. Small groups of five to six teachers should be formed for these interactions.

Brainstorming. Brainstorming, a valuable tool in creative problem solving and decision making, generates a large number of ideas. A warm-up brainstorm is helpful in freeing the mind from practical considerations and in encouraging fantasy. Possible topics for the warm-up brainstorms discussed by Gelatt, Varenhorst, Carey, and Miller (1973, pp. 30-31) are:

1. Ways to improve on the common bathtub (time limit: 4 minutes).

2. New kitchen appliances (time limit: 7 minutes).

After the initial warm-up activity, the facilitator may ask teachers to brainstorm good and then bad experiences they recall as elementary students. A discussion of good experiences reveals that special recognition, acceptance, or success were involved and resulted in positive feelings toward self and school. In contrast, bad experiences recalled from school days generally include embarassment, humiliation, failure, or isolation. This exercise has the potential of encouraging teachers toward more positive interactions with students.

Compare and contrast. Each small task group is instructed to identify terms and phrases defining open and closed educational systems according to the following four major headings: (a) learning theory, (b) curriculum, (c) instructional methods or techniques, and (d) evaluation procedures. Large group feedback follows. The differences identified by one group of teachers in an inservice meeting are included in Figure 6.

Incomplete sentences. Each task group is given two or three typical behavior problems encountered by teachers and asked to differentiate the handling of these problem by teachers functioning in an open and in a closed educational system. Examples of typical behavioral problems include running in the hall, habitual tardiness, willful disobedience, temper tantrums, rudeness, obscene notes, masturbation, petty thievery, defacing of school property, cheating, failure to pay attention, tattling, smoking, drug use, physical attacks on teachers, and lack of interest in classwork. Large group feedback follows. This particular exercise is facilitative in translating humanistic educational concepts into daily practice.

114

CLOSED SYSTEM	OPEN SYSTEM
LEARNING	
(Mechanistic theory)	Organismic (learning is
Connectionist theory	developmental)
S-R bond theory	Field theory (no area of
Conductionist theory	knowledge exists aside from
	all other areas of knowledge)
	Gestalt
	Trial-Error
	Perceptual
	Phenomenology
CURRICULUM	
Predetermined	Developmental
Logical	Emergent
Highly structured	Sociological
Reject experimentation	Psychological
Content-centered	Personal experience (student-
(Preparation for adult life)	centered)
	Dynamic
INSTRUCTION	
Deductive (Aristotle)	Inductive (Bacon)
Closed	Open questions with multiple
Indoctrination	answers
Transmission of facts	Inquiry
Imparting knowledge	Discovery
Limited question with	Exploration
predetermined answers	Experimentation
	Transactional (give and take)
	Interaction
	Experience
	Creativity
EVALUATION	
Facts	Critical thinking
Content	Problem solving
Doctrine	Use of rationale

Figure 6. Learning, curriculum, instruction, and evaluation in closed and open educational systems.

Phase II: Basic Beliefs and Personal Behaviors

Since teachers are dominant influences in classrooms, they must be encouraged to become cognizant of the influence of their belief systems on personal behaviors.

> Whatever we do in teaching depends upon what we think people are like. The goals we seek, the things we do, the judgments we make, even the experiments we are willing to try are determined by our beliefs about the nature of man and his capacities.... No beliefs will be more important to education than those we hold about the nature of man and the limits of his potential. Whenever our ideas about human capacities change, the goals of teaching must change, too. Whatever we decide is the best that man can become must necessarily set the goal of education. (Combs 1962, p. 1)

During this phase of the inservice, teachers are provided opportunities to examine what they believe about the nature of humans, how children learn, what constitutes a high-quality civilization, and what life skills are needed to participate in a high-quality civilization.

The nature of people. Each member of the small group is asked to complete the statement, "Mankind is basically..." (Stevens 1971, p. 245). After each member has completed that sentence, group members are instructed to substitute the words, "I am..." for "Mankind is basically..." and complete the second statement exactly as they did the first. After teachers have completed the second statement, they are asked to share their feelings about the substitution. This exercise generally produces an in-depth discussion concerning the nature of humans and the ramifications of the differing beliefs in daily educational practice.

How children learn. Each member of the small group completes the statement, "Children learn by...." Once again, group members are asked to substitute the words, "I learn by..." and to complete the second statement exactly as they did the first. Sharing feelings about this substitution produces a discussion and sharing of basic educational beliefs regarding the nature of motivation and learning.

What constitutes a high-quality civilization. Group members are instructed to state their beliefs concerning the characteristics of a high-quality society and then the characteristics of an undesirable society. Large group feedback stimulates discussion of this topic and the school's responsibilities in facilitating a high-quality society.

Basic life skills. Group members are asked to share their beliefs about the basic life skills needed to be participating members of a high-quality civilization. The discussion following this activity often leads to an examination of the curriculum presently being offered in the school. Is our curriculum offering students the skills needed to live in a high-quality society? Generally, the teachers recognize that they often emphasize the cognitive domain and almost totally ignore the affective dimensions such as loving, perceiving, valuing, and caring.

Phase III: Developing Authentic Human Communication

Study of human communications makes one painfully aware that many educators spend a great deal of time teaching children to read, write, listen, and speak but spend little time helping children communicate honestly with their fellow human beings. Taking time to facilitate authentic human communication, both verbal and nonverbal, is imperative in humanistic education. Therefore, teachers are encouraged to risk, trust, and share, to give and receive feedback concerning their own communication with others.

The following activities have proven helpful in enhancing authentic communication among several professional staffs. The teachers form small groups of five to six members for three interactions.

Nonverbal communication—Choosing a leader. Each small group is instructed to choose a leader without talking (Stevens 1971). Allow 3 to 5 minutes for this task. After each group has identified its leader, the members are asked to discuss the actual sequence of events resulting in their choice. They decide which group member actually took the most active part in choosing the leader. Of course, the member taking the most active part is the person who actually led in this situation, so he or she is the official leader of the group.

Verbal communication—Giving and receiving appreciation. One person moves a chair to the center of the circle and each member of the group tells two or three things that he or she appreciates about that person (Stevens 1971). Members are instructed that their comments may be as superficial or as deep as they like, but they must be honest. The discussion following this activity may center on these questions: Is it easy to express your liking? Can you accept and enjoy what others say to you? Were you phony in your expressions of liking?

Authentic communication—Parent and teacher conferences. Each small group of teachers is given background data on a child and is asked to select members to play the roles of the parent, teacher, child, counselor, administrator, or whomever is to be involved in the conferences. Videotaping of these role-play conferences is extremely useful for promoting sharing and self-evaluation by individual staff members.

Phase IV: Alternatives for Implementation

During this final phase of the inservice model, the staff is involved in the decision-making process. Educational decisions are made operational realities and then are implemented in the school. This systematic process of decision making focuses on the learner and the learning environment.

Figure 7 is a schema attempting to categorize the school experience. Operationally, the school consists of twelve components: (a) people, (b) human interactions, (c) curriculum, (d) organization, (e) team organization (optional), (f) instruction, (g) classification of pupils, (h) subject matter, (i) time, (j) space, (k) community relations, and (l) evaluation. Listed under each of these components are several existing possibilities for activation of the underlying assumptions of humanistic education.

As an example of the systematic process involved in decision making, one group of teachers selected the possibilities of self-assessment, descriptive and noncomparative, listed under the major component evaluation in Figure 7. They then selected complementary possibilities from each of the other major components and designed their school experience. The teachers then established priorities and beginning dates for implementation of these possibilities.

If past inservice education efforts have been more frustrating than satisfying, then perhaps it is time to consider the risk, trust, and share model.

People	Human Interaction	Curriculum	Team Organization	Organization	Instruction
Independent	Mutual respect	Child-centered	British infant	Temple City Model	Guide
Responsible	Sharing	Individual	Open	McKinney Model	Global goals
Intelligent	Trusting	Flexible	Nongraded	Joyce Model	Learning climate
Resourceful	Touching	Emergent	Continuous progress	Trump Model	Discovery
Self-motivated	Approving	Open-ended	Differentiated staffing	Allen Model	Inquiry
Cooperative	Genuine	Relevant	I.P.I.		Discussion
Curious	Authentic	Accessible	I.G.E.		Technology
Trustworthy	Compassionate	Activity	Multi-unit		Programmed instruction
	Warm	Experience	Multi-systems		Diagnostic teaching
	Empathic	Community-centered	Choice		Nonverbal and verbal communication
	Encouraging	Broad fields			Levels
	Caring	Self-contained			Interest
	Core	Departmentalization			Abilities
	Integrated	Contractual			Life-related

Figure 7. The educational experience.

119

Figure 7. The educational experience. (continued)

Classification of Pupils or Grouping	Subject Matter	Time	Community Space	Relations	Evaluation
Number of students in a unit	Cultural electives	Unstructured	Flexible	Publics involved	Open
Subschools	Cultural imperatives	Large blocks	Comfortable	students	Descriptive
Interage	Traditional	Smallblocks	Personal	teachers	Noncomparative
Family	Perceiving		Functional	administrators	Cooperative
Peer	Community		Quiet	parents	Letter grades
Buddy	Loving		Relaxed	community-at-large	Written
Interest	Knowing			Newsletter	Parent-student-teacher-conference
Skills	Decision making			Notes to parents	Profile sheets
Functional	Patterning			Verbal communication	Contracts
Achievement	Creating			Open house	
Independent study	Valuing				

References

Combs, A. W. (Ed.). (1962). Perceiving, behaving, becoming. Washington, DC: Association for Supervision and Curriculum Development.

Gelatt, H. B., Varenhorst, B., Carey, R., & Miller, G. P. (1973). Decisions and outcomes. New York: College Entrance Examination Board.

Goble, F. (1970). The third force. New York: Grossman.

Stevens, J. O. (1971). Awareness: Exploring, experimenting, experiencing. Moab, UT: Real People Press.

* *

Suggested Readings

Avila, D. L., & Combs, A. W. (1985). Perspectives on helping relationships and the helping professions. Boston: Allyn & Bacon.

Berman, L. (1967). New priorities in the curriculum. Columbus, OH: Charles E. Merrill.

Curwin, R. L., & Fuhrmann, B. S. (1975). Discovering your teaching self. Englewood Cliffs, NJ: Prentice-Hall.

Dobson, R., & Dobson, J. (1981). The language of schooling. Washington, DC: University Press of America.

Dobson, R. L., Dobson, J. E., & Kessinger, J. (1980). Staff development: A humanistic approach. Lanham, MD: University Press of America.

Dreikurs, R., Grunwald, B. B., & Pepper, F. C. (1971). Maintaining sanity in the classroom: Illustrated teaching techniques. New York: Harper & Row.

Glasser, W. (1969). Schools without failure. New York: Harper & Row.

Gouran, D. S. (1982). Making decisions in groups: Choices and consequences. Glenview, IL: Scott Foresman.

Moustakas, C. (1967). The authentic teacher. Cambridge, MA: Howard A. Doyle.

Moustakas, C. (1972). Teaching as learning. New York: Ballantine.

Purkey, W. W., & Novak, J. M. (1984). Inviting school success (2nd. ed.). Belmont, CA: Wadsworth.

Raths, L. E., Harmin, M., & Simon, S. B. (1966). Values and teaching. Columbus, OH: Charles E. Merrill.

Saint-Exupery, Antoine de. (1943). The little prince. New York: Harcourt, Brace & World.

Seaberg, D. G. (1974). The four faces of teaching: The role of the teacher in humanizing education. Pacific Palisades, CA: Goodyear.

SECTION V

EPILOGUE

EPILOGUE

Heisenberg (1958, p. 125) stated, "What we observe is not nature itself, but nature exposed to our method of questioning." As you have read through the previous chapters, it should be apparent that our world-view is influenced heavily by aesthetic, ethical, and political concerns. We have endorsed a particular set of values. That was our intent. As we stated earlier, decisions about curriculum, for example, why educators teach what they teach, the way they teach it, and to whom, are value based. All too often, under the guise of scholarship, educators are encouraged to write as if they had no presence in their works.

Throughout the book, we have made a major effort to confront the predominate technological mode of thought and discourse with a new framework for thinking and talking about children and the schooling experience. Rather than focusing on the isolated, procedural orientation of how to design and implement curriculum and pedagogical activity, we have attempted to assist the reader with an understanding of the personal, cultural, moral, and political consequences of curricular and instructional decisions. The intent was to further the work of other reconceptualist writers by exposing the ways in which societal patterns unconsciously are reproduced in schools and through this illumination, promote emancipatory activity (Mazza, 1982).

Inherent in the notion of creating a different framework for curriculum and pedagogical talk is the idea of development or gradual movement toward action. Of the visible reconceptualist writers, Macdonald (1975) explores most specifically the groundwork from which curriculum action might emerge. He believes curriculum action must take the form of praxis--action with reflection. This distinguishes praxis from activism (action without relfection) and intellectualism (reflection without action) (Freire, 1970).

Additionally, in the effort to suggest a new framework for curriculum and pedagogical thinking and talk, we have alluded that certain attributes of curriculum and instructional activity are treated in a problematic manner by those theorists subscribing to a technological mode. By problematic, we mean certain aspects of curriculum development and instructional improvement are ignored or receive only rudimentary treatment in a majority of theorists' writings. The critical omission is the neglect of axiological/aesthetic commentary. That curriculum development and instructional theory are fundamentally activities in expressing value theories and in making value judgments has been well documented (Apple, 1975; Macdonald, 1977a, 1977b; Pinar, 1981; Ubbelodhe, 1972/1973).

Dewey (1902) viewed the curriculum as a contrived environment. Macdonald's (1977b) interpretation of Dewey's concepts presents the school setting as a potentially manageable microcosm of a rather unmanageable macrocosmic society. In Chapter 7 we defined curriculum as an attempted interpretation of the human experience translated into educational specifications. Inherent in these conceptions of curriculum and instruction, or for that matter the whole affair of schooling, are broad questions of humanity. Macdonald (1977b, p. 11) states these questions; "What is the good society, what is a good life, and what is a good person?"

Elsewhere, we (Dobson, Dobson, & Koetting, 1984) have written extensively about other problematic aspects of schooling reform which tend to be treated in a casual manner. We contend there is:

1. An unwillingness to view recommendations for improving the nation's schools as being ideologically based. Are current recommendations for school reform supportive of a particular political climate?

2. An unwillingness of educators to concern themselves with ownership of the curriculum. Who determines what is basic or good for whom and for what reasons?

3. An unwillingness to deal with curriculum access when prescribing for improvement. Are the conditions of curriculum access prevailing in today's schools politically or ethically determined?

4. An unwillingness to admit that what happens in school, to, for, or with young people are value expressions. Is the claim of value neutrality in the guise of objectivity intellectually honest?

5. An unwillingness to recognize that the dominant perspective for problem solving, reductionism, too often results in simplistic solutions to complex questions. What are the historical/philosophical roots of the prevailing mode (technocratic rationale) for curriculum and pedagogical improvement?

6. An unwillingness to include in planning knowledge relative to the limitations of "objective" assessment tools. Has fascination with quantification as a reporting device encouraged the neglect of important aspects of schooling which tend to be qualitative in nature?

7. An unwillingness to recognize that schooling has become a highly mechanistic affair. Has the concern for efficiency resulted in curriculum and instructional programs based on a western industrial management model?

8. An unwillingness to entertain the idea that the planned curriculum has become a management tool. Is the

126

curriculum something to be mastered and measured or is it something to be lived and experienced?

9. An unwillingness to view schooling from a holistic perspective and to recognize that when one variable is altered all other variables in the network are affected. Can educators continue to deal with "particulars out of context" and expect any real improvement?

10. An unwillingness to recognize that "good" teaching and "good" curriculum are not a question of the right methods or content but have to do with teachers finding their own solutions to carrying out society's purpose. Is the historically and currently dominant technocratic-rationale grounded in solid educational research or is it based ideologically on the need to predict and to control?

11. An unwillingness to realize that the process (intent, values, knowledge base, etc.) through which interpretations of schooling are created is more influential than the interpretations themselves. What are the philosophical/historical roots of contemporary recommendations for school reform?

12. An unwillingness to see the curriculum and instructional program from a perspective of evolution. Do school leaders in positions of power possess a working knowledge of the curriculum and instructional ideas of past thinkers?

13. An unwillingness to consider metaphors for curriculum and instruction as ideologically based. Are metaphors borrowed from a military, medical, or an industrial model appropriate for talking about young people and the schooling experience?

If choices (decisions about schooling) made today serve to design the future, then we believe these problematic aspects must receive top priority in interpretations of past, present, and future schooling endeavors. Attributes associated with concepts such as ideology, values, process, and metaphors are complex in nature and difficult to deal with when creating scenarios and/or predictions.

We have questioned the folk wisdom of efficiency, control, and determinism. Reconceptual efforts can be understood as reflections of a shift in consciousness. Perhaps reconceptual efforts need to be directed toward facilitating a coming shift in the evolution of consciousness within a cultural frame of reference.

References

Apple, M. (1975). Commonsense categories and curriculum thought. In J. Macdonald & E. Zaret (Eds.), Schools in search of meaning (pp. 116-148). Washington, DC: Association of Supervision and Curriculum Development.

Dewey J. (1902). The child and the curriculum. Chicago: University of Chicago Press.

Dobson, R. L., Dobson, J. E., & Koetting, J. R. (1984). Problematic aspects of school reform. Unpublished manuscript, Oklahoma State University, Stillwater.

Freire, P. (1970) Pedagogy of the oppressed. New York: Seabury Press.

Heisenberg, W. (1958). Physics and philosophy. New York: Harper Torchbooks.

Macdonald, J. (1975). Curriculum Theory. In W. Pinar (Ed.), Curriculum theorizing: The reconceptualists (pp. 5-13). Berkeley: McCutchan.

Macdonald, J. (1977a). Values bases and issues for curriculum. In A. Molnar & J. Zahorich (Eds.), Curriculum theory (pp. 10-21). Washington, DC: Association of Supervision and Curriculum Development

Macdonald, J. (1977b, March). Looking toward the future in curriculum. Paper presented at the meeting of the Professors of Curriculum, Houston, TX.

Mazza, K. (1982). Reconceptual inquiry as an alternative mode of curriculum theory and practice: A critical study. Journal of Curriculum Theorizing, 4(1), 5-89.

Pinar, W. (1981). The reconceptualization of curriculum studies. In H. Giroux, A. Penna, & W. Pinar (Eds.), Curriculum and instruction (pp. 87-96). Berkeley: McCutchan.

Ubbelodhe, R. (1973). Axiological analysis and curriculum theorizing. (Doctoral dissertation, University of Wisconsin, Milwaukee, 1972). Dissertation Abstracts International, 33, 4254A.

SUBJECT INDEX